IRMA

Based On A True Story

Dennis Marsico

SYNOPSIS

Devin and Emily Marsden had battled hurricanes before in their long history of living in Central Florida. Seasons came and went and no storm really ever terrified them until September 2017 when Hurricane Irma made landfall on the peninsula.

As they prepared for the storm, they opened their doors to Devin's brother and his husband who were evacuating the southern part of the state and their coastal home. The Marsden's close neighbors who lived directly next to them in the suburban neighborhood, were the best neighbors anyone could ask for. With an imminent arrival of the storm and Devin's brother, husband and little dog on their way, they extended an invite to their neighbors. Alan and Jack and their new baby would join them for a small hurricane party to ride out the fierce cyclone heading their way.

Nothing would prepare them for what unfolded over the course of nine terrifying hours. The hurricane that raged outside became the least of their worries as they quickly realized the storm, they would fear the most, was inside their home.

Copyright
© Dennis Marsico 2023

All rights reserved, including the right to reproduce this book or portions thereof in any form whatsoever.

Dennis Marsico
Winter Garden FL 34787
United States
www.marsicocreative.com

For my entire family who support, encourage, inspire and most importantly, love me in ways I could ever merit. I reciprocate their love and support them with the same depth and sincerity. Jen, thanks for always being my anchor, my muse and as always, the voice of reason.

Contents

SYNOPSIS iii
PROLOGUE viii
CHAPTER 1 / BREWING 3
CHAPTER 2 / WAITING 11
CHAPTER 3 / SANCTUARY 22
CHAPTER 4 / ANTICIPATION 27
CHAPTER 5 / PREPARATION 34
CHAPTER 6 / IMMINENT 46
CHAPTER 7 / PANIC 56
CHAPTER 8 / RESERVATIONS 60
CHAPTER 9 / HUNKERING 66
CHAPTER 10 / ARRIVAL 76
CHAPTER 11 / HOUSEGUESTS 81
CHAPTER 12 / EFFECTS 95
CHAPTER 13 / POUNDING 106
CHAPTER 14 / GOODNIGHT 111
CHAPTER 15 / TERROR 120
CHAPTER 16 / FEAR 137
CHAPTER 17 / SURVIVAL 143
CHAPTER 18 / RELENTLESS 148
CHAPTER 19 / ADRENALINE 152

CHAPTER 20 / DAWN 155
CHAPTER 21 / AFTERMATH 159
CHAPTER 22 / EXHAUSTION 175
CHAPTER 23 / CLOSURE 180
EPILOGUE 190
ABOUT THE AUTHOR 195

PROLOGUE

The word hurricane derives from an indigenous word, *'hurakan'* coined by European travelers signifying evil spirits and weather gods that battered their ships in the Caribbean. Long before the presence of modern-day meteorologists, farmers would fear *'The Ala'*, a demon that would produce winds, hail and havoc that would destroy their crops. In Biblical terms the Hurricane wasn't necessarily an act of God, but more an act of the devil.

African folklore believes that storms forming off the west coast of the continent were spirits of their ancestors seeking revenge on their captors. Unprecedented storms are forming all the time in our oceans. Some say they are living and breathing and also form meteorological personalities. Storms also rage all around us, personally and spiritually. It is believed that intense storms can alter the state of mind and indirectly possess a soul.

"And once the storm is over you won't remember how you made it through, how you managed to survive. You won't even be sure whether the storm is really over. But one thing is certain. When you come out of the storm, you won't be the same person who walked in. That's what this storm is all about."
                              - Haruki Murakami

CHAPTER 1

BREWING

Devin heard the alarm go off but quickly hit the snooze button. He was already awake but foolishly thought that, in the extra six minutes his phone was allowing him to rest, he could go back into a deep slumber. He reached over to see if Emily was still in bed. He loved that feeling of touching her arm as she lay there sleeping. It was a reassurance and comfort that he loved, and he would touch her gently so as not to wake her. He knew the snooze would end any second, so he wanted to get his affectionate morning routine in before it did. He moved his hand closer to her and got a handful of hair. He thought that was odd, as he was always pretty accurate in finding her arm. He shifted and moved his hand down lower, only to find more hair. Before he knew it, a long, sloppy, wet tongue was licking him, and the breath of the dog wafted across his face. The alarm shouted at him again after the six-minute rest, and he quickly realized Emily was not beside him. He frantically hit the alarm again, but this time he turned it off, knowing that a snooze again would be pointless. Dude, their affectionate golden doodle that occupied Emily's spot in the bed, had already sprung to life. He loved to grab one of the hundreds of dog toys that were strewn about the house and say good morning. Today was no different, as he was already in Devin's face with a mangled Cookie Monster missing a leg and smelling like a combination of a dirty sock and a wet newspaper. Emily would religiously wash Dude's toys because of the pungent smells that would often radiate from them. He knew from the waft of Cookie Monster that it was time again to run his menagerie of toys through the washer.

Dude was one of the family members and not an ordinary dog. Devin had been reluctant to get another dog as the rest of the family waited patiently for him to say the word. Their former dog was perfection and would be hard to top. Once he realized he missed the companionship of a canine family member, he began research on various breeds. He landed on a golden doodle after reading that they didn't shed, made great pets, and were basically a person in a dog suit. When they found him, or more importantly, Dude found them, it was instant love. Garrett and Patty loved the curly fur ball and debated on names. After hearing Devin and Emily refer to the breed as Doodles, the kids thought that was the funniest name ever and began calling him Doods. Devin laughed after hearing that the first time, and Emily knew right away why. 'The Big Lebowski' was one of Devin's favorite movies, and having a dog named Dude gave him complete joy. The kids didn't get it, but it didn't matter. To them, Dude was Dude because he was a golden doodle. Dude was fun, loyal, and goofy, and he fit in appropriately with the family.

After Dude greeted him, he heard the shower running in the bathroom. Emily had obviously been up and started her day. It was not surprising, as Devin was amazed at how his wife could function with little to no sleep. Her herculean feats of working full time, tending to the kids, cooking, and endlessly washing dog toys would exhaust anyone. It's not that she didn't want to sleep; it was just that she couldn't. She notoriously worried, as many mothers do, about everything, and she would often toss and turn in bed. Most nights, Devin would wake up and see the glow of her phone as she scrolled through TikTok videos to keep her mind off things. Devin was equally committed to keeping the household running as smoothly as possible and helped in any way he could. Outside yard work was his domain, but he also helped inside the house when he could. Emily appreciated it, but Devin never thought it was enough to take even some of the burden off of her.

Devin stumbled into the kitchen and poured a cup of coffee. He was going to pour a cup for Emily but saw that the carafe had some missing already and knew she had already had a cup, most likely within arm's reach on her side of the sink in the bathroom. He let Dude out for his morning pee, let him back in, filled his bowl up with food, and headed back into the room. Their morning routine would be to turn on the news and catch the headlines before the day started to get ahead of them. Devin turned on the news and pushed pause to wait for Emily to come out of the shower. She would like to see the headlines and check the weather before getting Garrett off to school and heading to work. As Devin waited, he checked his phone for any messages or emails. He was alarmed when he saw all the weather notifications that were displayed across his screen. Another storm was close to being named, and the local weather teams were all abuzz. They had been following it, but it was too early to tell where this one was headed. Hurricanes or tropical storms that were on a path anywhere near the state would cause a feeding frenzy of panic. It was like throwing chum into the proverbial waters and watching the shark's attack. Devin and Emily had become numb to the number of storms they had been through over the years. Major storms that caused them to board up their house or pull in some pool furniture, but nothing apocalyptic. Emily's mother, however, would always think the worst and would begin the hourly phone calls. Her mother was a worrier too, a true testament to genetics, and would watch the news from Connecticut. Emily would have to constantly reassure her that they had been through these storms before and they would be fine.

Emily emerged from the bathroom in her robe with her hair wrapped in a towel. Devin smiled and said, "Good morning, beautiful" (a term of endearment he would always use) and made his way to her to give her a kiss.

"You were up early," he said.

She responded and said, "Once again, my mind was racing. I have so much to do at work this week, and I am completely overwhelmed. I saw on my weather app that they don't know where this storm is headed. Did you wake up, Garrett, yet?" Emily would often be a run-on sentence of anxiousness, and Devin would always tease her about it.

"Which worry should we tackle first?"

"Well, how about waking up our son? That's a good start."

"I will. We have a few minutes. Let's watch the headlines, and I'll go up and wake him."

Devin pushed play on the remote, and the headlines came on as they sat back in bed, sipping on their coffee. The typical news stories were blathered about: crises in the Middle East, political strife at home, rising house prices, and a plethora of bad news that made Devin question why they even continued to watch each morning.

Dude hopped back on the bed and curled up next to Emily. She looked at him, almost envious that he could just doze back to sleep so easily, as she patted his head. The broadcaster announced that a look at the weather was coming up. Devin turned to Emily and said, "My phone blew up last night with weather alerts. I guess this storm is brewing." She glanced at the phone and said, "Mine too. That's one of the things that kept me up last night."

The complacency in Florida when storms approached was rampant. Two weeks of hype and preparation for these storms were exhausting. The weather folks are warning residents to stay alert and diligent and not to let their guards down. There was almost disappointment in their voices, as many times at the last minute, a high front would steer it away from the state, or a low front would weaken it or oddly steer it closer. Whenever these fronts collided with a storm, it would either help or hinder the storms. This is why Floridians only paid attention to pending storms until the absolute last minute. A never-ending game of meteorological chicken.

The national news, which Devin turned on in the morning religiously, had its eye on the storm that was brewing in the eastern Atlantic Ocean. Usually, that meant that it could be worth looking at and maybe paying a little more attention compared to what they had in the past. Local news always seemed ready to broadcast twenty-four hours a day and saturate the airways with any and all updates. To be fair, the storms should be taken seriously, but Devin and Emily knew which ones to pay attention to and which ones were hype. Emily watched intently as the news showed the possible paths of what had become a massive storm overnight.

Emily said, "It looks like this could be a serious one." Devin looked at her and said, 'Don't they say that about all of them?"

"Stop. Why do you do that?" Emily quipped.

"Do what?" Devin innocently responded.

She said, "Downplay every storm. I mean, yes, some are hype, but this one seems serious."

Devin heard in her voice that she was worried and knew none of his sarcastic remarks or jokes would be welcomed.

"All we can do is keep watching and see what path it could stay on. You know how unpredictable these things are.

Besides, they are saying it's too early to tell, and we'll have time to prepare if we have to."

Emily got up and headed out of the bedroom. Devin knew she was done with him and didn't comfort her at all. He heard her head up the stairs to wake Garrett up. It wasn't easy waking a 5th grader up each day. Patty was at least at college and, therefore, made life a little easier at home, reducing the task of waking two groggy kids each morning.

They had been through this routine before with their three older boys when they were younger and were now reliving it with Garett.

Devin stayed glued to the television as he listened to the coverage of the storm. What had only been a tropical depression well to the south of Florida's peninsula yesterday had developed into an official tropical storm in six hours. The forecaster bellowed from the television's speakers, "This is one to take seriously, folks. It looks like she's gaining strength quickly. We are waiting on the latest advisory from the national weather service. The agreed models are keeping it south but heading west, expected to turn north after it skirts Cuba, but it's still about 650 miles southwest of the Cabo Verde Islands."

Devin was glad Emily was out of the room. She didn't need to hear any of this to add to her stress. He looked at his calendar on his phone to see what meetings he had today. August 31st, 2017 showed three Zoom calls. Just as he lifted his head from his phone, the lead meteorologist from the local station was now on the screen, pointing at the studio green screen with a massive, angry storm in the ocean.

"It's official, folks; this beast has grown dramatically, and now it is our ninth named tropical storm this season. Say hello to Irma."

CHAPTER 2

WAITING

The next day started out like all the other days in the Marsden household. Devin let Dude out, had coffee in bed with Emily, and Emily felt surprisingly rested that morning. This was surprising since the night before, she had stayed up a little late to check Patty's location at college. Patty had gone to a party, and Emily could rest easier once she knew Patty had made it back to her dorm. Once confirmed on her phone, Emily fell asleep quickly. She planned to touch base with Patty later today, as she always did. Emily was a great mom, nurturing the family in a way that left Devin in awe. When they first met, they had both been divorced. Emily had never had children in her first marriage, but Devin came with three incredible boys whom Emily cared for and loved as if they were her own. Patrick, Thomas, and Joseph, or Pat, Tommy, and Joey, as they were affectionately called, adapted quickly to their new stepmother since they were so young when Devin and Emily got married. Devin's ex-wife and Emily always got along, often ganging up against him. They all managed to make it work, and it was considered the healthiest environment for all the kids. When Emily wanted more kids, Devin thought, what was one more after having three? When they discovered they were having a girl, Emily wanted to name her after her grandmother, Patricia. The family joked about having a boy named Patrick and a girl named Patricia. Pat and Patty would later tease each other, claiming they were the favorite "Pat" in the family.

Patty was born, and Devin had to readjust to raising a girl, something foreign to him. All was complete with their extended family until eight years later when Garrett came along. Now, they were beginning again, but everything fell into place. Garrett, being a boy, was more familiar territory to Devin. The stress of having five children weighed heavily on Devin, while Emily happily embraced every moment. An eternal optimist, Devin needed that in his life. He was convinced that when Garrett was in Emily's womb, he sensed that he was the fifth and last child, so he better be an easy child. He was, and Devin was relieved and grateful.

The talk of the storm that filled the airwaves wasn't on their minds anymore. They knew they had days to watch it and needed to continue the daily functionality of their lives. Emily got ready for work as Devin was on Garrett duty, getting him off to school. Luckily, Garrett's school was about a five-minute walk or a three-minute bike ride away. Devin helped Garrett pack up his backpack, and Emily made sure he had his lunch. Emily still had a few things to do before heading to work. As she kissed Garrett goodbye and gave him his daily hug, Devin watched him head down the sidewalk to elementary school. Once he rounded the corner, he would meet up with his friends and pedal the rest of the way with them.

Devin worked from home, so his routine wasn't as involved as the rest of the house. He had worked for so long in the corporate world for a major event company, consulting and training executives on how to be better public speakers, presenters, and overall performers. When the company was rumored to be downsizing, Devin became proactive and took the leap to start his own business. He was frightened at first but never looked back. Emily was ready to go and head out the door. Devin walked her out, as he often did each day. He pushed the button to open the garage door and watched it rise to expose the bright Florida sunshine. As it opened, he noticed a set of legs standing in the driveway. When the door fully opened, he realized their neighbor Alan was standing there.

"I was just about to ring your doorbell when I heard the garage door opening," Alan explained.

"Good morning, Alan," Emily responded in her normal cheerful tone when it came to the neighbors, or anyone she would say hi to.

Devin chimed in and said, "Good morning, neighbor. Do you need something?"

Their neighbors, Alan and Jack, were incredible people and easy to get along with. When Emily and Devin moved in, Alan and Jack had already been in their house for a few years. They had just adopted a little girl and could not be more excited. Devin would always tell Emily how lucky they were to have great neighbors. It became a typical stereotypical suburbia relationship: shared dinners, cookouts, chatting across fences, borrowing items, and just overall friendship.

Alan said, "I hate to bother you, but Jack forgot to get milk for the baby last night, and we need a cup to hold us over."

"I am on my way to work, but I am sure my stay-at-home husband would be happy to oblige," Emily said jokingly.

"You two are the best!" Alan squealed.

"Well, one of us is." Devin quipped back.

Emily rolled her eyes, as she often did at Devin, but he became accustomed to it when the inevitable joke or teasing would always come out of his mouth.

"How is Sloan, by the way?" Emily asked Alan, referring to their newly adopted nine-month-old adopted child.

"She is so precious! We can't take our eyes off of her, and we just hold her and stare at her for what seems like hours." Emily gave him a huge smile, followed by a sigh. She knew the exact feeling and relived it for a moment.

Alan quickly chimed in and said, "Oh, before I forget, are you following the storm? It's named now. Irma, is it? Who thinks of these names? It sounds like an aunt from the turn of the century. They are hyping this thing up so much, but it could be days from now before we know."

"I hate how the weathermen feed on all of this," Devin said.

Emily knew she was about to be caught in one of Devin's diatribes about weathermen, hurricanes, and storms and said, "We are watching it, but right now all we can do is wait and see." She glanced at her watch and gasped. "Oh my gosh, I am so late! I really have to go."

She gave Devin a quick kiss and said a fast goodbye to Alan. She got in her car and drove out of the driveway as Alan stepped to the side. She gave another quick wave to Alan, then blew another kiss to Devin and drove off.

"Let me grab that milk for you," Devin said.

Alan jumped in and said, "Oh, wait here, you can put it in this," and handed him a baby bottle he had tucked under his arm.

"Do you want to come in while I get the milk?" Devin asked Alan.

"No, Jack is waiting for me because I yelled at him for forgetting to buy milk last night, and I told him he was going to the store first thing this morning to get some. He is so scattered-brained."

Devin laughed and continued into the house. Jack was pretty scattered-brained and sometimes a little goofy, but they were both good people, and Emily and Devin adored them. Devin grabbed the milk, poured it into the bottle, and headed back outside. When he arrived back at Alan, Jack was standing there holding Sloan, who was dressed in a beautiful little pink dress. They loved being new parents, and it seemed like on some days they would put various outfits on her. Emily would always joke with Devin, that they must have a walk-in closet full of little girls clothes. Sloan was a little irritable, which could only be from her hunger as she waited for her dad to settle the milk issue. Jack handed Sloan to Alan as he tried to settle her. Devin could barely give the bottle to Alan as Sloan quickly grabbed it and placed it in her mouth.

Alan jumped in, turned to Jack, and said, "See how hungry she is? If you remembered to get milk last night, she wouldn't have been starving." Devin thought it was a little bit of a harsh tone and an overreaction, but he could see why Alan was frustrated. He had also been on the receiving end of that frustration from Emily when he was tasked with picking something up from the store but forgot to.

Jack turned to Devin and gave a nervous smile, then said, "Good morning, Devin. Sorry, you had to see that." Devin could tell he was half-joking but also a little embarrassed after being scolded by Alan in front of him.

"Hey, no worries. I'm sure you guys have heard the wrath of Emily from your house yelling at me, even with all your windows closed and the TV on." Devin was stretching the truth, of course, to make Jack feel better, but he was glad Emily wasn't there to hear that. He could somehow still feel Emily's glare or customary eye roll, even if she was long on her way to work.

Alan looked at Jack and said, "Ok, enough chitchat. You need to get to the store." Jack nodded and began to walk to his car in the driveway. Before he could reach their driveway, he turned on his heels and said, "Are you guys keeping an eye on the storm?"

Alan quickly answered for Devin and yelled. " YES! They are watching it like everyone else! Now get to the store!" Alan realized he was probably too blunt again and added, "I love you!" Jack smiled, hopped in the car, and drove off.

"Honestly, I love him, but I swear he would forget his head if it wasn't attached to him," Alan said feeling the need to justify his treatment of Jack.

"No need to explain. We all get a little flighty from time to time." Devin responded.

Alan brought the focus back to the storm and said, "Well, let us know if you hear any new updates on the storm."

Devin said, "Turn on any of the stations, and you will see something on them." They have already started their panic broadcasting. It's too early to tell, but they are worried about some of the models."

"Mmmmmmm, back in my single days, I was always worried about the models. Especially the ones in tight jeans." Alan couldn't resist the joke as Devin politely laughed.

Devin decided to quip back with a Dad joke and said, "Well, on that note, I have to start my long commute to work."

Devin was the king of dad jokes, although that one landed flat as Alan just stared at him and, after a short pause, said, "Alright, neighbor, thank you for the milk. Sloan, thanks to you as well." He lifted her little foot and shook it like he was waving her hand since she didn't have one free as she clutched her bottle of milk. Alan began to walk back to his house. He turned to Devin and said, "Let's plan a dinner or drinks… or something, or all of the above, soon."

Devin said, "Absolutely, we would love that."

Devin headed into the house, went into the office, and turned on his computer to begin work. Just to have some white noise in the background, he also turned on the weather channel. He doesn't usually overly worry about these storms, but something about this one seemed different. The Tom Petty song lyrics flashed in his head: 'The waiting is the hardest part.'

From a distance, he thought he heard his mother calling but stopped his friends from making noise as they played in the sparkling cave by the edge of the forest. The winds were building on the island, but that was typical of living in the eastern Caribbean. He knew the winds howling through the caves could sometimes play tricks on your ears. After a brief pause in play, he knew it was the island speaking and not his mother. Herberto was only twelve years old but was considered to be a friend to both young and old on the small

island. Barbuda was all he knew, and he seemed to know everyone. The island was only 62 square miles, so it wasn't unheard of to see the same people all of the time. He was such a happy kid that his nickname was 'Hapberto'. So many of the locals never understood how he could be so happy since his father passed away when he was eight. A senseless death from the flu that went ignored until it was too late That left just him and his mother in a tiny shack on the edge of his little coastal town. His mother would sell painted shells to the many tourists who would pass through, and it seemed to be enough to get by. Herberto was her world, and he adored his mother. In his little heart, he vowed to stay happy for her after his dad was gone. He loved to play in the island caves, and he knew how to navigate them with his friends. His mother would worry, but she knew it made him happy as he played each day after he had done his chores and schoolwork. Herberto was particularly happy that day. Earlier, on his way to meet his friends, he stopped and helped a local farmer herd some of his goats that had gotten loose. The frustrated farmer recognized Herberto because he would pass by his place every day, smiling, singing, and sometimes laughing. The local farm produced some cotton but also had some livestock and chickens that would often roam freely but sometimes stray a little too far.

Today the farmer was glad Herberto's routine was the same, as he needed the extra pair of hands to guide the animals back to an acceptable designated area. Once Herberto was finished and helped him get all the furry fugitives back near his property, the farmer thanked him. He then produced a wrinkled dollar from his wallet and noticed it had a small smiley face drawn on it. Obviously, a doodle from the previous owner of the bill. It was an ironic little compensation for the happy boy. The smile that developed on Herberto's face when the farmer handed it to him could have been seen from space. He couldn't believe it.

"Gracias señor!" He shouted. The farmer smiled and said, "It is my pleasure, my friend. You have helped me tremendously today, and you should be rewarded. The animals are restless as they sense the storm is close by." Herberto wasn't really sure what the farmer was talking about and, frankly, didn't care. He and his mother did not have a television. If anything, important was happening, they would often find out through neighbors or other locals. A chain of communication that would make its way around the island. Everyone seemed to look out for one another, and any impending threats to the island were usually communicated by word of mouth. They knew how to handle storms and were no strangers to them. The farmer had a radio that looked like it could have been from the 1950s but still worked and was his source of any forecasts that could affect his crops and animals. The farmer knew Herberto was only interested in the dollar he had handed him and looked at him and said, "You should head home soon, Herberto; they say the storm is moving quickly." Herberto managed to break free from his gaze at his reward and replied.

"Other than some wind, sir, the skies seem clear."

The farmer looked down at him and said, "La Calma antes de la tormenta" (The calm before the storm). Herberto knew he was keeping his friends waiting and headed off. As he skipped off, the farmer shouted, "Be careful, my friend! Let your *mother know the storm is growing!" Herberto could only focus on getting to his friends. Just then, a cloud that had been threatening to block the sun covered it, and it began to rain slightly as the wind howled through the trees. The farmer's animals began to make a cacophony of sounds, and it startled him. He looked to the skies and whispered under his breath, "Irma estas enojada" (Irma, you are angry).*

CHAPTER 3

SANCTUARY

Emily started her daily journey to work. She always seemed to have so much on her mind, but the respite in the car on the way gave her time to breathe a bit. She could listen to a plethora of stations that the satellite radio would provide, but most of the time she would call her mother, her father, and often Patty to see how college was going. She was, in fact, the queen of nurturing and taking care of people. This benevolent care spilled over into her job as executive director of an animal shelter and animal rights center. She had worked there for over twenty years. She was overworked and underpaid but never complained. It wasn't about the money; it was about taking care of not only the animals but also the staff that worked for her. All of her employees loved Emily, and rightfully so. She was kind, understanding, and a great champion for them.

As Emily continued to drive, she accessed the radio channel through the convenient button on the steering column of the car. She landed on one of the many news channels, as once again they were discussing the storm. Emily knew she had some time before she arrived at work to make a phone call. The dilemma was, who was she going to call? Although her parents lived in the same house, they were in their own worlds. They each had their own cell phone and only sometimes shared the call when Emily reached out to them. If she called her dad to check in, it could lead to a thirty-minute discussion on the weather, and with the buzz about the possible storm coming, that could be a much longer call than she was prepared for. Her dad loved to talk about the weather. He knew cold fronts, high pressure, low pressure, barometric pressure, and even had a rain gauge attached to his house. Devin would always joke and say it was a geriatric rite of passage to talk about the weather. If she opted to call her mom, that could go either way. If her mother was in the mood to talk, it usually led to ninety percent about her and would only allow for ten percent of Emily's update. Emily didn't care, though. She allowed everyone to do their thing as she willingly listened. She made the decision to call Patty because she wanted to hear her voice. Just as she was about to make the call, her phone rang, and the car speakers shouted at her, "Incoming call from Patty." Emily was relieved but not surprised, as it happened so often. They would both always exclaim that they were just about to call each other. Emily quickly hit the accept call button.

"Hi, baby girl." It was Emily's nickname for Patty since she was a baby, and she, of course, would always say, "I was just about to call you!"

"Hi Mom!" Patty's voice was upbeat and cheerful, just what Emily needed to hear.

"How was your night last night?" Emily asked

"It was great! I was able to get some studying done, and then a group of us headed to Zee Zee's."

Zee Zee's was a notoriously famous chicken joint located just off campus, near the university. Every time Devin, Emily, and Garrett visited Tennessee, Patty would take them there to eat.

Emily jumped in and said, "What about the party? Did you go?"

"Yes, we went for a bit but ended up leaving because it was lame. That's why we went to Zee Zee's," Patty responded.

"Well, as long as you had a good night, I see that you got home around midnight." Emily confidently stated that she checked her location on her phone.

Patty laughed and said, "Yes, stalker mom, that's about right!"

Emily loved the tracker capability on her phone. She would often joke and say she wanted to see where all the kids were at any given moment. Devin would tell her, "That's not what it's for, and our grown adult children don't need to be tracked." He would laugh at her, but he knew it was her nurturing nature and her concern for all the kids. Her heart was in the right place, and Devin was lucky to have a wife and mother to their children like Emily.

Patty changed the subject and said, "What's going on with the storm? You guys worried?"

"Yes and no," Emily replied. "You know how these storms are. They may or may not stay on the forecasted track. Either way, we will be ready. In the next couple of days, we will have a better idea, and I will make a run to the store. I'm not looking forward to that with all the crazy people buying everything off the shelves."

Florida was known for a rush on stores before every hurricane. Essentials were important, but the amount of water and toilet paper people would unnecessarily buy became so cliche. Devin would always say, "There could be an impending apocalypse, and people still wouldn't buy as much compared to an approaching hurricane!"

Emily was pulling into work and knew she had to get off the phone with Patty. They said their goodbyes and hung up, knowing they would talk again before the day ended. Emily pulled into the parking lot and into her space. She may not have been paid what she was worth, but dammit, she earned her own parking space. There in front of her, mounted on the pole, stated, 'Emily Marsden, Executive Director'. She was proud of that. She was proud of her family. A smile came across her face. All five of their kids were doing great. The age gap between all of them was comical, but she didn't care. She had a special place in her heart for all of them. Pat and Joey were in Vegas and doing well with their jobs and girlfriends, and Tommy lived close by with his wife Nicole and their little boy, Levi, Emily, and Devin's first grandchild. Life was good. Great family, great job, great husband, great dog, great neighbors. The radio was still on as Emily was about to turn off the car. The radio blared about staying tuned for an update on the storm. Emily looked up and saw one of her coworkers waving her inside, indicating some sort of work-related fire Emily would have to put out. She couldn't bear hearing another report about the storm, so she turned the radio off and indicated to her coworker that she would be right there. As she grabbed her bag, her coffee spilled a bit from the travel mug she always had by her side in her car. She sighed a heavy sigh and opened the door, leaving her little vehicular sanctuary and headed into the building.

CHAPTER 4

ANTICIPATION

There are so many constants in Florida that you could set your watch to. Turn signals that remained on from senior citizens failing to realize it was flashing for thirty miles, the excessive heat in the summer, mosquitoes, tourists, and the inevitable hurricane season that runs from June 1st through November 30th every year. Despite all of these annoyances, the Marsden family loved living in Florida. They grew up in the cold up north but had lived here for so long that they preferred the heat. There were plenty of positive things about living in the sunshine state, and they took advantage of it whenever they could.

A few days had passed, and Devin and Emily were looking forward to a couple of days off together. Garrett had a long weekend coming up, and school would be closed on Monday for Labor Day. Garrett had every school holiday marked on the calendar and loved days off from school. He enjoyed being in fifth grade but also loved hanging out with his friends on the weekends and taking extra days off from education. Devin and Emily liked the short school weeks probably even more as it allowed for one less day of the week; they would have to deal with school preparation. One less lunch to worry about, one less school outfit to pick out, and one less night of homework. Vowing to keep the weather and news to a minimum over the weekend, Devin and Emily thought it would be great to take a road trip with Garrett to the beach for a couple of days. An overnight trip could be fun and just what they needed to take their minds off things. Garrett would often get anxious whenever storms hit. It was bad enough that they had a dog that would stress every time thunder was close by; they also had to comfort Garrett when an afternoon thunderstorm hit.

Devin always thought that Garrett inherited his mother's tendency to worry and learned to live with it. Patty didn't seem to have it as much and seemed a little more carefree.

Devin began to make a list of beach necessities that he would have to gather from the garage, while Emily made a shopping list for snacks and lunches. Devin found a great little Air B&B that allowed dogs, so Dude could go as well. Garrett was excited and was looking forward to a fun trip to the beach. It was one of his favorite places to be and one of the only places where he wouldn't be glued to his phone. Garrett had asked if Zack could go with them as well. Zack was Garrett's best friend, and they did everything together. Zack had become an honorary family member, and Devin and Emily welcomed him over at any time. The beach trip was no different, and they made arrangements for Zack to join them on their weekend adventure.

Devin was looking forward to long naps on the beach, and Emily couldn't wait to sit by the water in her favorite beach chair and get lost in a good book. They needed a couple of days of no distractions and relaxation. They knew if they stayed home on the weekend, they would get caught up in the mundane chores of keeping the house together. Cleaning, mowing the lawn, and laundry. In the grand scheme of things, all things could wait.

Garrett, after getting approval for Zack to go with them, asked if he could ride his bike over to his house. The two fifth graders had to make lists of their own. It was important to list what balls they would bring, which boogie board worked best, and what snacks they wanted. Devin was in fifth grade ages ago and knew that the talk of girls at the beach was probably on their list of topics as well. Garrett biked off to Zack's house, which was just a few blocks over, and could ride on the sidewalk the entire way. Once Devin saw him around the corner, he went back inside to continue their beach planning with Emily. As he walked inside, every phone began to ring or had some alert sounding off.

Emily had her personal phone and a work phone. Devin had two phones as well. They also had a landline. House phones were as ancient as eight-track cassette players, but Devin and Emily kept one. They always joked that not even Emily's parents had a land line anymore. They vowed to get rid of it, but since it cost them practically nothing, they kept it in the house. Even the house phone was sounding off. A perfect storm of ringtones and alerts
"My god!" Devin shouted, followed by, "What the hell is going on?" At that point, Emily had emerged from the kitchen holding three phones, all yelling at her. Devin grabbed his two phones from the counter and glanced

down. All of them had a test from the emergency broadcast system coming from them. Just as Emily looked at hers, she noticed that it was odd that the house phone was ringing at the same time. She placed the screaming cellphones down and grabbed the house phone. The display showed Helen Galloway. Emily's mother. She answered the phone, as the cellphones were all still blasting the alarms.
"Good timing, Mom." Emily half-joked. Her mother, hearing the ear-pitching sounds coming from the other phones, immediately shouted, "What the hell is happening down there? Are those emergency alarms?"

"Yes Mom. Just a test of the emergency broadcast system. Had this been an actual emergency, an official message would have followed the tone of alert you heard at the start of this message." Emily laughed and was proud of herself for making the joke. Devin immediately got it and doubled over in laughter. Emily heard silence on the other end of the line, then her mother said,
"What? I don't get it. What are you talking about?"

Emily tried to explain, "It's what the computerized voice says when we get alerts or emergency calls from..." Emily stopped herself, realized it was futile to try to explain the joke, and just carried on. "What is it, Mom? Everything alright?"

"Yes, but we are watching the weather channel and are concerned with the path of this storm," Emily's mom said with concern. Emily knew it wasn't really her mom watching the weather channel but her dad giving her mother a play-by-play. Emily foolishly thought for a few hours that she could avoid the mention of storms or hurricanes, but no luck. Emily's mom continued.

"Your father saw the computer models, and they are all aligning. It's supposed to hit the Eastern Caribbean and then move up by Cuba, then south Florida, and possibly right up the center of the state near you."

Devin heard all of this since Emily always had her mother on speaker phone. By now, the emergency alerts had calmed down on the other phones, but what suddenly caught Devin's attention was Emily's mother's mention of a possible strike in south Florida. Devin's brother Bill and his husband, Pete, lived in South Florida. He knew he needed to call them and check in. They had just built a house, and Devin knew a direct hit from the storm could be rough.

Devin glanced at his phone again and saw a rip tide alert at local beaches over the weekend. Up and down the coast, there were dangerous rip tides forming and possible beach erosion. Shit, he thought. There goes our trip to the beach.

The anticipation of a weekend beach getaway turned into anticipation of a major hurricane.

Marisol was elated to start her new job. Cuba had been her home for so long, and finding a job as a transportation assistant was not easy. After graduating from college, she

vowed she would help her family as much as she could. She was the oldest child of six siblings, and living in Cuba had not been easy. Through hard work and determination, she landed a job quickly and would start work soon. Her new position was based at the Naval Supply Systems Command in Guantanamo. The job seemed simple enough: compiling shipping documents to finalize goods and items being sent out. Tracking and managing transportation systems and dealing with customer concerns was something she was looking forward to. The only concern she had with the job was that it was relatively far from her home in Moa, where she still lived with her parents. The journey each day would involve a quick taxi ride and then a bus ride to Guantanamo.

Marisol was a planner and knew she would need to map out a route and have a strategy to make this work. In Cuba, you never turned down a job because of the distance. You took the work when you could get it and figured everything else out later. Since she had a few days before her new job would start, she would do a few mock runs to her new job from her home. Timing every moment from when she got up, when she showered, when she ate breakfast, and when she needed to leave the house. The local taxi was easy, and she could access it with a quick four-block walk from her house since that was the holding area for the local taxis and rideshares. After a twenty-minute cab ride, she would arrive at the bus station, where she should hop on her next leg of transportation to get her job. The bus would only take about 35 to 40 minutes. After mapping and planning, Marisol tested the route the next day. She woke up as if it were a work day, showered, ate, left the house, and headed to the taxi. The taxi picked her up and drove the short ride to the bus station, where she happily

hopped on. The driver smiled and greeted her as she sat down directly behind him. The bus had other passengers, but they were spread out in various seats. Marisol was so happy that her routine was falling into place. She knew this could work each day if she allowed enough time in the mornings. The bus departed the station and drove down the windy Cuban terrain. Marisol, during the ride, would glance at her watch, calculating the timing and marking it down. She was diligent about planning and making this work. The bus continued around a curvy stretch of road as it passed by an older abandoned apartment building on the side of a hill. Marisol marveled at the dilapidated structure. She was amazed that it was still standing and looked like it could crumble at any moment down the steep terrain. As the bus slowly approached the curve, Marisol could see the ocean and knew they were getting close to Guantanamo. As the bus driver battled the giant steering wheel, the bus shifted a bit from a gust of wind that quickly came off the sea. It was quick and violent and rocked the bus back and forth. Marisol and the other passengers were a bit alarmed, but the bus quickly settled back into place. Marisol could see the bus driver in the mirror as sweat was running down his face. Sitting behind him, she heard him say under his breath, "Irma estas haciendo que los vientos sean malvados como el diablo."
(Irma, you are making the winds evil like the devil.)

CHAPTER 5

PREPARATION

Devin broke the news to Garrett about the beach trip being canceled. He expected more disappointment from him, but Garrett could find just as much joy staying in the neighborhood and hanging out with all of his friends. The riptides and dangerous currents were nothing to mess around with in Florida, and it was crazy to risk a trip to the beach. Emily and Devin promised Garrett they would reschedule and possibly make it on a weekend when Patty was home from college. That made Garrett happy, and he continued to call Zack to break the news to him.

By now, the breaking news all over the state was that all the computer models were agreeing with each other that Irma was on a path to hit Florida, possibly in about six to seven days. The interesting thing about storms in Florida is that residents eerily seem to keep calling it 'the storm' until it is officially projected to hit the state, and then it is called more often by its name. It was almost as if once the storm was officially named and its direction wasn't clear, it became a Harry Potter moment. 'He (or she) who must not be named!' Perhaps adding a bit of magic to it and steering it away if you didn't call the storm by name. That notion went out the window as the state started preparing for the possible direct impacts of a Category 5 hurricane. Hurricanes always fluctuated as they approached. Some retained their strength, while others sizzled out. They were like living beings, and their fuel to keep them moving and alive was the warm waters of the Atlantic or the Gulf of Mexico. Devin was about to make the call to his brother in Naples when the Ring Doorbell alerted him. Emily was in the bedroom, first on the phone with Patty, then with her mother. Her mother was, of course, panicking and projecting impending doom, which, of course, would make Emily even more anxious. It always baffled Devin how Emily's mom could live in Connecticut and appear to have her finger on the pulse of a hurricane that wasn't even affecting her and was twelve hundred miles away. Then Devin realized it was easy with Emily's armchair meteorologist dad in the house.

Devin opened the front door and almost knocked over his neighbor. Jack was standing there with a plate of cookies. Devin always hated the fact that the front door opened out. It was an odd feature on the house when they bought it, but they realized builders installed them to prevent strong winds or even burglary attempts from pushing in the door. He vowed to change it ever since they moved in, but it became lower and lower on the project list.

Jack immediately said, "Ok. I just wanted to thank you both for the milk the other day. I was so scatter-brained and forgot to pick it up for the baby. Alan was so mad at me, as you probably noticed, but here is a peace offering, and again, thank you."

Jack handed Devin the obviously chocolate-chip cookies that he could see through the cellophane over the plate. Devin said, "Jack, this is so unnecessary. We always have milk in the house, and you are always welcome to have it. It really wasn't a problem."

"You guys are just the best. Good neighbors are so hard to come by, and we always talk about how great you both are," Jack said sheepishly. He often seemed like a bit of an enigma to Devin. Jack could often be a bit socially awkward and, at times, never really look you in the eye. It wasn't a major problem or issue for Devin, but he could never quite put his finger on it. Devin thought it must be hard not only to be a gay couple but now to adopt a little girl. The hurdles and obstacles they had to overcome, not to mention the prejudice, must be exhausting. Alan and Jack never felt that from Devin and Emily, as they were absolutely accepting of all lifestyles. Devin early on told them both that he, in fact, had a gay brother, and that seemed to put their minds at ease. It shouldn't make a difference, but in this day and age and with so much hatred, it was important to Devin and Emily that they knew they were accepted. There were other neighbors at the end of the street that Alan and Jack would have hated living next to, based on the vile and hateful bumper stickers that would adorn their cars. Devin would often walk Dude past their house and just be disgusted by it. They would always smile, wave, and say hello. Devin smiled and would wave back, knowing it was all fake. It didn't matter because Devin and Emily lived in the best part of the cul-de-sac and were equally happy living next door to Alan and Jack.

Devin stood there holding the cookies and said, "Well, we both thank you and truly appreciate it. These will not go to waste." (as he patted and pointed at his waist.) Devin smiled, but only got a stare from Jack. Another dad joke had gone down in flames.

"Well, let us know if you need anything, and hopefully this crazy hurricane will pass us, and we can all do dinner," Jack said as he began to walk off the porch.

"Ok, Jack, thanks again," Devin said as he was shutting the door. Just then, Jack blurted out,

"Oh, one more thing. I made the cookies, and I always like to have just the right portion of chocolate chips in each one, so hopefully they are all good. It helps that the ratio is balanced when dipping them in milk."

Devin paused for a second, not quite knowing how to react, then said, "I'm sure they are fine, Jack," then officially shut the door. Devin again thought to himself that Jack was an odd guy.

Emily came out of the bedroom looking exhausted, which she sometimes did after conversations with her mother. She immediately said to Devin,

"My god, between my father playing Al Roker and my mother being, well, Mother Nature, I'm done!"

Devin leaned in to hug her, and Emily willingly accepted. She needed a good hug. Devin said, "You know how your mother gets. She's a worrier like you."

Emily knew Devin was right, but it was so frustrating for her. She knew her mother cared, but it was the way she went about caring that sometimes drove Emily crazy. This wasn't the first time they had to deal with Emily's mom and hurricanes. One year, three hurricanes in a row hit the state, all within three weeks of one another. Her mother was a wreck then and even insisted that Emily and the kids check into a hotel to be safe while Devin stayed at the house. In one of the storms, they all evacuated and hit the incredibly packed highways, as everyone in the state had the same idea to flee. They sat in traffic for hours and fought long lines at gas stations. After the mayhem, confusion, and exhaustion from three storms in a row, Devin vowed never again to evacuate or hide in a hotel. He felt it was more dangerous to be on the roads, and the possibility of getting stuck on a freeway as the storm approached was more daunting than staying at home. It's better to hunker down in your house and wait it out. If they lived on the coast, it might be a different story, but being so far inland, most of the time they were protected.

After comforting Emily after her traumatic phone call, Devin knew he had to make a call to his brother. There had been enough distractions, and the conversation between the two siblings needed to happen. Devin grabbed his phone and dialed Bill's number. The phone rang twice, and Bill picked up and said, "Hello, little brother." Bill seemed oddly chipper considering a hurricane could potentially strike them within the week.

"Hey there," Devin replied. "You guys are preparing for the storm? What's the plan?"

Bill got distracted for a moment and yelled to Pete in the other room, who was searching for his glasses. "They are on your head, love! Sorry, Devin, a small crisis was averted. We were just talking about our plan. We weren't too concerned, but looking at the path of this monster, we are thinking of packing up and hitting the road for a few days." Devin knew that was probably a good idea, as the latest models had it passing right over where Bill and Pete lived.

Bill and Pete moved from Ohio to Florida five years prior. Bill had just retired as an administrator from the local government office in Akron. Pete was a systems analyst for a chemical company and retired as well. Devin was told on countless occasions what Pete's actual job entailed, but he could never remember the details. It was all too complicated and scientific. Devin spoke softly into the phone because he knew Garrett was close by and didn't want him to hear and cause him any more anxiety.

"Listen, Bill, I think it's best that you guys evacuate. It looks like Irma is going to be in category five when it hits. Your house is in the crosshairs. Why don't you leave in enough time so you can stay with us? We are far enough inland and are as prepared as we could be. Emily and I talked it over and want you to come."

The truth was, they weren't really prepared yet, and Devin and Emily hadn't discussed having houseguests yet. He knew Emily wouldn't care because she adored Bill and Pete, and them staying at the house to ride out the storm would not be an issue. Bill responded, "I told Pete that we could always stay with you because we have Bella." Bella was their miniature poodle and was always welcome when they came. Dude loved her, and it was like a canine sleepover with treats, walks, and ball-throwing.

Bill continued talking, now lowering his tone as for Pete not to hear, "He is so stubborn. He wants to drive as far north as we can, probably out of the state, near the border line. He says we will find a hotel and be safe there."

Devin spoke next and added his experience from their previous hurricane road trip years ago "Bill, you guys can do what you want, but the roads that far north will be jammed. We tried that before a few years ago, and it was hell. It's better to ride it out here."

Bill chimed in, "You're preaching to the choir, brother. Pete is nervous; it's going to be bad everywhere, not just the coast near us."

"Look, even if it does come over us, you know as well as I do, they lose some of their steam coming across the state." Devin said. "We will make a little hurricane party out of it."

By then, Pete was yelling from the other room after watching the latest weather update. He was insisting Bill get off the phone, as he was getting nervous and needed to start making plans and preparations to leave.

Bill said, "Look, I have to go. We will keep you posted. I have to look up hotels and see if we can book something, maybe near Georgia. It will make him feel better. If anything changes, I will call you. I love you, Devin. Stay safe."

"I love you too, Bill. Talk soon," Devin replied, and he hung up the phone.

Devin knew they had to start preparing as well. Emily was already one step ahead of him, cross-checking her shopping list with what was on Alexa already. As Emily asked Alexa what was on her shopping list, she responded in her robotic tone and spouted off the items. Devin walked into the kitchen and said, "The storm is getting stronger. Bill and Pete are evacuating." Emily looked at Devin with worry in her eyes. Garrett was in the living room watching television, and they didn't want him to hear their discussion. Just then Alexa sprang to life and broadcast throughout the house, 'Would you like to hear the latest update on Hurricane Irma?'

Devin and Emily simultaneously yelled, 'ALEXA, NO!"

Captain Barry's Fishing Charters was one of the highest-rated fishing excursions, according to Yelp reviews, in the Florida

Keys. The owner, Barry Wittleson, was a salty old ex-Navy sailor who made the sea his home. He didn't have a fleet of boats like other charter companies. His forty-foot boat was popular among local fishermen and tourists due to its large size, facilities, and guarantee of a return home with fish. The day-long charters he provided were enough to keep a roof over his head and cover his living expenses. He lived simply and had no family that anyone knew of. One day, he arrived in the Florida Keys and set up his life. He never talked about where he came from or his background, and the locals learned quickly not to ask. He lived in a local trailer park close to the marina but would often spend the night on his boat, as he felt most at home there. The trailer was mainly to have a mailing address for his business and to store any supplies he couldn't fit on 'Hook Em', the name of his vessel. His appearance was rough, and his demeanor was sometimes harsh, but his ability to navigate the waters and know exactly where the fish were was unprecedented and well known.

The rate he charged covered gear, a bagged lunch, and, for an extra charge, cleaning and gutting your catch. Captain Barry would pay local high school kids to clean the catch on the docks, and the partnership seemed to work out fine. Barry also had a deal with the local owner of the cafe. They would bag up lunches for his passengers and drop them off at the pier each morning in a large cooler for him to load on the boat before the passengers arrived.

It was a simple and easy setup, and Captain Barry paid everyone in cash. He hated technology, the banks, social media, computers, and pretty much anything post-1951. He didn't even have sonar on his boat to locate schools of fish because, in his eyes, that was cheating. He was seventy-two years old and set in his ways. Fishing and making money from it were all he knew.

One thing Captain Barry discovered, or, some say, invented, was a particular kind of pump for smaller boats. He was an engineer in the Navy and was incredibly good with his hands. When he was just starting out, he had a small boat and was limited in the number of fishermen he could take. The boat could never seem to drain the water properly after a thunderstorm. Larger boats like 'Hook Em' have bilge pumps built in and can automatically pump the water out in case of flooding. When Captain Barry arrived one day at the dock, he noticed his small boat listing to one side. Water had poured in from the storm the night before and threw his little vessel off kilter.

After analyzing the situation, Captain Barry devised some sort of contraption that could sense when the boat began to list, turn on a small pump, and extract the water. It was a homemade contraption, but it seemed to work beautifully as he tested it during the typical afternoon thunderstorms that plagued Florida in the summer. Other mariners would walk by his boat, see the contraption, and ask him how it worked. Captain Barry wasn't much for long conversations and told them in as few little words as possible. "Balanced weights, gravity, hose pieces, and a little bit of electricity." He grumbled at the passersby. There were some at the marina who thought if he could make it a little more sophisticated, it could be patented, marketed, and sold to boaters worldwide. Captain Barry had no time for that and was not the least bit interested. The extent of his invention went as far as a few other boaters at the dock that needed the same help. As gruff as he was, he befriended a few other fishermen and saw the need to help them with his contraption. He was lucky enough not to need it on his newer boat and thought, What the hell? He would make a few for those with smaller boats.

The day ended like any other day after returning on the 'Hook Em' with a full load of passengers and fish. Some of the passengers were a little green around the gills. A few of them got sick about halfway through as the impending storm was churning up the waters fiercely. Usually, this would mean that there were a few extra-bagged lunches in the cooler. When you were seasick and puking over the side of a boat, the last thing you wanted was a bagged lunch. Captain Barry would give the free chow to the local fish cleaners as a little extra bonus for them on some days. The local kids began their routine of gutting and cleaning fish, and Captain Barry began the clean-up and prepared his boat for tomorrow's excursion. He could always tell it was a successful fishing day as he watched and listened to the multitude of seagulls squawking around the dock sinks as the catch was cleaned. As the captain began his end-of-day chores, the marina master mariner (a term used for the marina owner) came over the loudspeakers that were placed all around the docks.

"Attention boaters. Due to Hurricane Irma and her approach, we are asking all mariners to secure their boats and, if necessary, begin procedures to remove them from their slips."

Captain Barry listened to the announcement and laughed to himself. Bullshit, he thought. He would secure his boat but not remove it. It was absurd. A boat was meant for the water, and the 'Hook Em' would remain in her slip. He would tie down *what needed to be tied down, secure items in place, or remove them if needed, but his baby would stay put. He had been through numerous storms with his smaller boat as the years passed, and it always survived the turmoil. He knew some of the other less experienced boaters would need his assistance, and for some of the few, he rigged up his contraption.*

Captain Barry had seen it all. He fought in wars, was out to sea for months at a time, and weathered many hardships. He wasn't worried about this storm. He never was, except for the one thing that caught his attention that day. He had never experienced this before, and some say that if you did, the storm that was approaching was going to be bad. Captain Barry looked over to the sinks as the kids cleaned the fish. The kids looked as baffled as he did. There were no seagulls scrounging for scraps and filling the air with an orchestra of bird calls. The air was silent. Captain Barry looked to the sky and said, "Irma, you are a bitch."

CHAPTER 6

IMMINENT

It was the night of September 5th, and all the computer models were in agreement by this point. Irma was heading directly towards the Leeward Islands, then would power past Puerto Rico, skirt Cuba, bounce off the Florida Keys, and then up the state. Forecasters were calling for a landfall in some locations as a category five, then only dropping to a category four once it hit the peninsula. Devin had begun the initial work to prepare the outside. This would include the normal routine of gathering the pool furniture, pool toys, umbrella, and anything else he thought might fly away in over one hundred-mile-hour wind gusts. Devin and Emily specifically purchased a house with a pool. It was on Devin's list of must-haves when the initial house hunting began for them. Their house before didn't have one but had a community pool. Emily was content with the neighborhood pool, but Devin became tired of lugging everything there, fighting for a spot, and dealing with the occasional pool closing due to exploding diapers. At first, Emily wasn't thrilled about a pool, but once they moved in, she quickly learned to love the idea. There was something to be said about opening the sliding glass door and walking right out into your own oasis. Most Florida pools had screened cages around them to keep out the bugs, which is exactly what they had.

Emily's daunting task of battling the insanity of the grocery stores was done. She hated dealing with the craziness of Florida grocery stores when a hurricane was approaching. She managed to come out unscathed and stock up the house in preparation for Irma.

Devin had prepared Emily for a possible visit from his brother and Pete if the evacuation to a hotel didn't pan out for them. Emily was worried about them on the road and was insisting that they come to the house and stay. They still had a few days to decide but needed to act soon since it was forecast to hit the Florida Keys on September 10th. Naples and South Florida would feel the effects shortly after that. Emily, being the nurturer, kept bugging Devin to call Bill and insist that they come to the house and not go to a hotel. He told her he would continue to try, but he knew how stubborn Pete could be. Once he set his mind to something, it wasn't easy to change it.

The biggest challenge was keeping Garrett calm as they waited for the storm. They did their best to shield him from any unnecessary worry, but he heard enough excitement and chatter at school. They were already flooding parents' phones with messages on how the county and the school district were preparing and would take precautions for the children's safety. Devin and Emily knew the schools would close, but Irma could be a weekend storm. As anxious as Garrett would get, he was still a kid in school, and any chance for an extra day or two off was more than welcomed.

Devin was hungry from rearranging the entire outside pool deck and staging in by the sliding glass doors. He had learned from storms in the past that even though they were predicting a direct hit, they could shift at the last minute and miss them entirely. He would meticulously prepare the outside potential projectiles by the door. Once he knew for sure that the storm was on its way, he would move everything inside the dining room area, right by the kitchen. It was all one big gathering space that Emily loved when they had company over, or all the kids and their grandchild. The kitchen and large table all flowed together. She even added a little couch in the corner because she knew the kitchen was always the gathering place. She loved to cook and loved having her family surround her when she did. The large kitchen counter, the dining room table, and the comfy little sofa made it the perfect gathering spot.

Devin made his way into the kitchen to search for food. He knew there were a plethora of things to choose from because of Emily's outing to the grocery store the day before. Emily was at work, Garrett was at school, and his meetings were light that day, which is why he got a jump on storm prep. As he opened the pantry to begin his quest, his phone rang. He looked at the display and saw that it was Emily.

He picked up the phone and said, "Well, hello there. Did you miss me so much you couldn't stand it anymore and just had to call me?" Emily was so used to Devin's attempts at any type of humor that most of the time she ignored him. He did make her laugh, though. A lot. That was one of the things that she loved about him. When she had an agenda and time was limited, most of the time she plowed over him and ignored his feeble attempt at being funny. This was one of those times when she said, "Are you raiding the pantry? Don't break into those snacks yet. I bought them for the storm, so we have stuff to munch on."

Devin was always amazed at her ability to call and know when he was about to eat something he shouldn't. He responded and said, "I'm not. I was just grabbing something to drink," as he placed the bag of potato chips carefully back on the shelf so she wouldn't hear the bag rustling.

"Did you call your brother again?" She spoke.

"Em... I did it twice. If they decide they are leaving, and I believe they are, they are attempting to book a hotel."

She quickly responded and said, "Well, that's absurd. They are never going to find anything if they wait too late."

Devin tried to calm her and said, "Look, let it happen then. If they get stuck and can't find a place, they can always come here."

His response seemed to set her mind at ease for a moment. She then said, "Hey, I saw Alan and Jack today when I was leaving for work. I told them, As the storm gets closer, maybe we could have a little hurricane party."

Devin laughed and replied, "That's funny. That's what I told my brother. Is that some sort of lighthouse beacon for gay men? A promise of drinks and light fare during a storm?"

Emily said, "Oh my god, that's horrible."

Devin quickly thought, "Speaking of which, if we do end up hosting a hurricane gathering, I probably should grab some more liquor." Devin and Emily weren't huge drinkers. Devin would indulge in a greater variety of drinks than Emily. He liked beer, wine, and an occasional martini. He even recently started to drink more whiskey, even though, after a hard night of drinking Jack Daniels in college, he vowed never to touch whiskey again. Emily would drink wine from time to time and, on rare occasions, something stronger.

Emily said, "Well, if you have time today or tomorrow, run out to the store and grab whatever alcohol you think we need."
"Ok," Devin replied. "If my brother does end up coming, he will probably bring ingredients for cosmopolitans. He never leaves home without them."

Emily chuckled and needed to hang up. They said their goodbyes, and Devin continued his search for something to eat. As he looked deep into the pantry, his phone alerted him. He glanced at his phone, and it displayed another weather alert. It read, 'Hurricane Irma is approaching the Leeward Islands. A direct strike is imminent.'

The farmer looked out of his window after hearing the constant banging of a tree branch against his house. He was frustrated with himself, as he had many times meant to trim the tree back but always got distracted with other projects. It was impossible to try and do it now with Irma bearing down on the island. The winds were fierce and the rain was steady as the violent storm introduced herself to Barbuda and the locals who called it home. The farmer's house was simple, but like many of the small dwellings on the island, it was built with cement blocks that held up well in storms. He also had a large enough barn to house the animals that he acquired over the years. Luckily, before Irma approached, he made sure his livestock, chickens, and cats were all accounted for. He was safely settled in and sat at his kitchen table with a warm cup of tea as he listed the weather reports on his small little radio that had become his only companion. Every so often, the radio would cut out after a particularly strong gust. Between the static of the radio and the constant knocking of the tree branch against his house, it was difficult to concentrate. The few feral cats that he acquired were safely in the barn. They were good to have around, as they became his personal exterminators, keeping the field mice away. The other two-house cats he had by his side would add to the collection of sounds as they meowed, listening to the fury outside.

As the farmer got up to prepare another cup of tea for himself, he heard the banging again. This time, the banging sounded different from the annoying branch that kept making itself known. As he moved towards the stove, the banging became louder, and this time it was accompanied by almost a wail. He looked at his two cats, who lay there on the kitchen floor and were, for once, silent. The farmer then realized the sound was coming from his front door. He made his way to the window and tried to peer out but could not see far as the rain was coming down hard at this point. He got closer to the door and knew right away that someone was banging furiously and yelling. The farmer carefully unlocked the door and opened it, slowly bracing himself against it as the wind was forcing its way in. As he opened it a little further, he saw a woman standing there. She was soaked and could barely speak. He knew right away that the wailing he heard was from her as she tried to get his attention to open the door. He immediately pulled her in as she collapsed in his arms. When she looked up at him, he recognized her. She looked familiar. Then it occurred to him. She was the happy boy's mother. Herberto, the little boy who skipped by his farm almost daily and helped him recently gather the animals for him, had seen the boy's mother before in town and on other occasions, but she mostly kept to herself.

She composed herself and tried to speak but needed a moment to catch her breath. When she was ready, she looked at the farmer and said, "Has vista a mi hijito, Herberto? (Have you seen my little boy, Herberto?) Herberto would always regale his mother about his adventurous days and would mention the farmer's house often. It brought him joy to pass by and see the animals.

The farmer knew why the woman was hysterical. She was out in this storm looking for her son. What mother wouldn't be frantic? He sat her down and explained that he had been by the other day on his way to see his friends and that he had helped the farmer collect his animals that had gone astray. The mother, still sobbing, said, "He was home last night but must have gotten up early and left this morning."

The farmer looked at her and said, "Did he not know about the storm?"

She said, "Yes, yes, but he wanted to explore again with his friends today, and I told him he had to stay home. He knew I was sleeping and must have snuck out."

The farmer tried to calm the mother and said, "It's ok. The boy knows this island better than anyone, and I am sure he is somewhere safe. Let me make you a cup of tea, and I will look for him."

The farmer did as he promised and made her a cup of tea. He even got her a blanket to wrap herself in. Her clothes were soaked, and he hoped the blanket along with the tea would help to warm her up. The farmer grabbed his raincoat and put on his boots. He knew she would be safe and could breathe for a moment while he went out.

He was surprised that the power was still on because, in past storms, the island grid would always fail right as a storm approached. Just as this crossed his mind, the power flickered and went out. Fortunately, it was daylight, but the storm made his house dark. He grabbed a candle for the boy's mother and lit it. She barely could hold her head up, and when she made eye contact with him, she sobbed, "Encontrar a mi chico" (Find my boy.)

The farmer opened the door quickly and ventured outside in the howling winds. He had a plan of attack and knew where to search first. Down the road, about three hundred yards, was a small path that led to one of the many popular caves that littered the island. This particular one was very popular with the local children as it offered a small, shallow pool for swimming, good shelter from the rain, and natural geological shelves that acted as seats.

He knew Herberto would frequent this cave with the other children. The farmer thought it would have been fun to explore the caves if he had been younger. The labyrinth of hidden caves acted almost like the arteries of the island. The tides would come in and fill the caves, and then, as quickly as they filled, they would rush out. Many of them were safe to pass through, and some even offered large ledges to walk on and away from the water. Many of the local children used them as shortcuts, cutting off twenty minutes, in some cases, on their journey around the island.

The farmer knew how to navigate in the wind and had to be vigilant as he saw debris starting to swirl around. He kept his head down and plowed through the torrential rain until he arrived at the path that led down to the cave.

He made his way down the path and remembered thinking about how his trusty boots were being put to the test as he carefully walked down the muddy path towards the cave. As he got closer, he thought he heard the cry of a young child. He listened carefully, trying to block out the wind and the stinging rain that was hitting his face relentlessly. He pushed forward and arrived at the entrance of the cave as the yelling became louder. He looked to his left at the cave opening and heard the howl of the winds emanating from it. It suddenly occurred to him that the wind swirling through the caves was the voice he was hearing. An eerie summoning. The water was rushing in and out of the cave violently and taking on a life of its own. As a huge spray of water came crashing over the farmer, he turned his head to shield himself. As the water subsided, he saw to his right the tide pool, which often acted as the local swimming hole. It was churning angrily as well, but something caught the farmer's eye. A large clump of twigs and leaves had gathered in the surging waters. As he looked closer, it wasn't just the leaves and debris that caught his attention, but the figure of a small boy. He was face down and floating, with his arms spread out as if he were almost flying and not floating. The farmer got close to the edge and grabbed the boy by his shirt. He pulled him to the small bank by the cave and reluctantly turned him over. As he did, he knew immediately that it was Herberto. The once-happy little boy was now lifeless. As the farmer looked closer, he saw, floating next to him, the dollar that he had given the boy a few days ago for his help finding his animals. He also looked closely at his face, and through the pelts of rain, he could see the once happy little boy still somehow had a slight smile on his face. Irma had taken her first life.

CHAPTER 7

PANIC

As Hurricane Irma was becoming more alive, the state was on high alert. Food, supplies, and generators were flying off the shelves. Devin and Emily stayed tuned in as weather reports were constantly updated. Devin would always recall the famous Ben Franklin phrase, 'Nothing is certain except death and taxes'. As a hurricane approached, he always wanted to change it to, 'Nothing is certain except death, taxes, and the insanity that ensued at Florida grocery stores before a storm.'

Fortunately, Emily had a jump on the mayhem at the stores. They were sufficiently stocked, and Devin had a chance to grab some extra wine and beer just to have on hand. They had shielded Garrett as much as they could from any details about the path of Irma. The meteorologists were hoping for a front to come down and push her away, but at this point in the forecast, this wasn't going to be the scenario. Garrett hadn't been shielded at school and was hearing all the buzz, including the rumors of schools being closed. They knew he would be okay, but the hype of the storms was often worse than the storms themselves.

Devin and Emily let him go about his daily routine, which included hanging out with his friends before the storm got closer. Garrett had asked them earlier if he could go to Zack's house and hang out. They both told him he could go for a bit. Garrett got his bike out of the garage and drove off for the short ride to Zack's.

As he biked away, Emily jumped as Alexa shouted at them. 'Hurricane Irma is expected to hit the state of Florida within 48 hours. Would you like to hear the latest track?'

Emily jumped and said, "Oh my god! I hate when she does that!"

Emily was famously and easily scared, and Devin often relished in it. He loved scaring her, sometimes intentionally, for a laugh. Most of the time, however, it wasn't intentional. Devin could walk out of the room and walk back in, and Emily would jump out of her skin. This was a daily occurrence to which Devin had grown accustomed.

They decided to ignore Alexa's request and turn on the weather channel to get the latest on Irma. They planted themselves on the sofa and watched the live update.

The forecast was becoming more and more consistent, and all the computer models were in agreement now. The storm was coming up from the bottom of the state and heading towards the interior. As the myriad of weather professionals spouted their opinions on Irma, Emily looked over to Devin and said, "Your brother has to come here. Look at the path. It's going right over them. They would be much safer here, but they need to leave soon."

Devin wasn't about to argue. He switched from the weather channel to the local news and saw they were broadcasting remotely from various locations. Some journalists were at gas stations reporting the long lines to get fuel; others were at home improvement stores watching plywood fly off the shelves. One reporter was just off the interstate, announcing that the roads looked clear now but soon would lock up due to evacuations from south Florida. The state was in turmoil, and Devin grabbed his phone and immediately called his brother.

The phone only rang once, and Bill picked it up immediately. There wasn't even a hello when Bill jumped in and said, "Christ, this hurricane is driving me crazy. Pete is demanding we leave, and I have been on the phone for three hours trying to find a hotel."

Devin knew this was useless after hearing the evacuation orders come in for south Florida. He said to Bill, "Why does this surprise you? Everyone is evacuating and heading north. There are no hotels available within five hundred miles."

At this point, Bill was only half listening and yelling at Pete about what they needed to pack for their road trip. "Do you really need to bring all those clothes?" Bill quipped. "We are evacuating from a hurricane and not going to Fire Island for the weekend."

Devin chuckled and said, "Look, you guys can do what you want, but have you seen the cars starting to hit the road? It's a nightmare. If you leave first thing in the morning, you can be with us in four hours."

"I keep telling Pete that," Bill grunted. "He thinks if we make it to Georgia, we will have a better chance of getting a hotel."

Devin said, "Georgia?" How long do you think it will take you to get there? On a normal day, you can hit the state line from where you are in about nine hours. How long do you think it will take tomorrow? It's insanity to try and attempt that."

Bill said, "I know. We have the news on now, and the evacuation orders have been widened to other areas."

No sooner did those words come out of Bill's mouth when he heard Pete yell from the other room, "Never mind, we are going to Devin and Emily's!"

From the other end of the phone line, Devin heard Bill say, "Oh shit They just showed some of the highway cameras going north. This is not looking good. People are starting to panic. We are leaving today. I'll call you on the road," and he hung up.

CHAPTER 8

RESERVATIONS

Emily was relieved after hearing that Bill, Pete, and Bella were on their way to take refuge in their house. It would worry her too much knowing they were driving aimlessly to find a hotel and possibly getting stuck on the road somewhere in the middle of a hurricane. Dude overheard Devin tell Emily that the three of them were coming, but all that Dude heard was 'Bella.' He got overly excited, and Devin had to reassure him that it would be soon but not yet. That didn't stop Dude from marching over to the window and to begin the wait for his little canine cousin.

Devin knew if Bill and Pete left soon, it could still take them a while with all the traffic, but they would still beat the storm. The house was prepped and fully stocked. Devin made sure every flashlight had batteries, ice was bagged just in case they needed to throw food in a cooler, and all possible projectiles were brought in from outside. Devin's staging area, right outside the door, was no longer there. After seeing the storm updates, he brought everything right inside the house so as not to take any chances. Even though they were inland, a strong enough hurricane could still do some damage.

Garrett was prepared too. He had all his favorite snacks that Emily had bought him; he charged all his electronic devices and downloaded some new games. He even appeased Emily and put two books and a flashlight by his bed, knowing full well that the books would probably remain unread. Devin thought it would be fun to get Garrett and Zack walkie-talkies so they could communicate as long as they possibly could during the storm. Since Zack was right around the corner, she was hoping it was within range. Garrett gave Zack his walkie-talkie, and they tested it out. Out of precaution and to prepare for evacuees, the schools closed a day early. Garrett and Zack were constantly calling each other with the signal button on the front. "Calling Irma Central, this is Zack One," the walkie-talkie blurted out.

Garrett replied, "This is Irma Central; go ahead, Zack One." Devin laughed. Why they were Irma Central, he wasn't sure. Maybe because they were housing his uncles during the storm and were fully supplied with snacks, flashlights, candles, weather radios, and anything else storm prep-related that you could think of. All he knew was that it was keeping Garrett occupied and his mind off the storm, even though he deemed his house, Irma Central.

The barrage of phone calls began earlier in the day and didn't stop. Emily's mom called at least four times, wanting to know the latest update every second. Emily's twin brother and only sibling lived in Boston. He was calm and level-headed and checked in once, making sure that they were okay and ready. He was a good guy, and since he lived closer to Emily's mom in Connecticut, he would run interference and help calm her down when storms like this would approach Emily, Devin, and the kids. He and his wife and two kids would visit every couple of years, and it was always a good time.

In addition to his brother Bill, Devin had two sisters who lived in the Cleveland, Ohio, area with their families, not far from where they all grew up. They all checked in, but most of the time when Devin talked to his sisters, it turned into a laugh fest. The hurricane was only talked about for a moment, and then, with all of them, it turned into a reconnection moment. Devin and his siblings lost their parents years ago in a freak accident on a road trip back from the Catskills. An icy road, a truck, and a crash. Gone in an instant and a blow to the family, Devin and his siblings relied on one another and kept moving forward. Any time to reconnect with all of them was a good time. Storm or no storm.

The phone calls continued as Emily's phone once again came to life. This time, it was Patty. "Mom, what is happening? The hurricane is looking bad. Are you guys, okay?" Patty quickly blurted out a run-on sentence.

Emily said, "Honey, we are fine. We are prepped and as ready as we can be. Your father got everything in from outside; I went grocery shopping. We are good."

Patty replied, "I feel like I should drive home and be with you guys." Patty barely had time to say anything else when Emily said, "Absolutely not. You are safe where you are. The storm is barely going to be a storm by the time it hits you, and you are in a dorm room. You cannot and should not drive here."

Patty knew she was right. It just worried her, and she needed to feel like she was somehow helping. Maybe by offering to come home, it would fill that need.

Emily changed the subject and said, "Your Uncle Bill and Uncle Pete are coming, though."

Patty said, "Oh, good! They live on the water, so that makes sense. Plus, I saw on the news that Irma is expected to go right over where they live."

"It took some convincing, but they agreed and are on their way," Emily said.

"How's Garrett?" Patty asked eagerly.

"He's good. He is ready, and Zack and him are chatting away on walkie-talkies," Emily replied.

"Oh, how cute!" Patty said.

Emily and Patty chatted longer, and it was just what Emily needed after fielding so many hurricane-related calls. Patty filled Emily in on school, boyfriend drama, clothing purchases, and the newest menu item at Zee Zee's.

Emily told Patty they would keep her posted as the storm approached. I love you's were exchanged, and they ended the call. As Emily hung up the phone, the doorbell rang. She heard Devin head to the door, then heard their neighbor Alan greet him as he opened the door.

"Hi there, neighbor!" Alan said.

Emily made her way to the foyer and met Devin.

Alan continued, "Well, hello there, Emily."

"Hi, Alan," Emily replied.

Devin said, "What's up, neighbor?"

Alan anxiously said, "Well, I am preparing for the storm, and Jack is still at work. Can I trouble you, Devin, to help me move our patio table inside?"

"No problem," Devin responded. "Let me put on a pair of shoes. I'll be right back."

As Devin left, Emily continued the conversation.

"Devin's brother and his husband are on their way from South Florida. Since they are being evacuated, we told them to stay here with us to ride the storm out. As I mentioned before, maybe you, Jack, and Sloan can come over tomorrow. You can meet Bill and Pete. We can have some cocktails and maybe some snacks. You know, a little hurricane party!"

Devin had returned from getting his shoes and said, "What's this I hear about a hurricane party?"

Emily said, "I reminded Alan and Jack about drinks tomorrow."

"I'm not going to argue with that," Devin agreed.

Alan said, "Oh, I love that! Sounds good."

Emily said, "So I can put you down for 6:30 tomorrow night?"

"Confirm our reservations! See you then," Alan said cheerfully.

Devin and Alan headed off to move the table. As Emily shut the door, she jumped three feet off the ground as Alexa said, "Did I hear you want to make reservations? I can help with that."

Emily shouted, "ALEXA STOP!"

CHAPTER 9

HUNKERING

Devin had finished helping Alan move his table inside the house and walked back over to his yard. He sat on his porch as he glanced at his phone and saw two missed calls from Pat and Joe. His two oldest sons always checked in weekly, but they knew they were calling to see what was happening with the storm. He dialed Joe's number first since he knew he could probably catch him at home. There was a three-hour time difference, and he did the math. It was one o'clock there. It was still early enough to talk with them both. Devin had always been in awe of his kids. They were all so different, but they were all doing well and were happy. Pat moved to Vegas first, then Joe followed.

Pat had started his own company as a performance consultant similar to what Devin did. He would train executives and company presidents and guide them on how to perform and talk in front of crowds. Joe was a talented video director and moved to Vegas to work with Pat and his clients. It all seemed to work, and they were happy in Vegas, but Devin and Emily missed them and loved any chance they could get to see them.

The phone rang for a bit, and just as Devin was about to hang up, Joe picked up.

"Hi Dad! How's it going?"

"Hey there, son!" Devin said it with a smile. "Are you working today?"

Joe jumped in and said, "Yes, but not until later. I'm filming a dinner event, and one of Pat's clients is speaking. I'm in the office now, getting things organized. Hey, how's the storm prep going? Are you guys going to be, okay? Is Emily nervous?"

The boys, as Emily called them, knew she would get nervous but knew her worry and concern always came out of love. Emily completely embraced the boys when she married Devin and helped raise them.

Devin responded to Joe and said, "Yes, we are all a little nervous about this one, but we will be okay. Uncle Bill and Uncle Pete are coming to stay with us to ride the storm out."

"Oh, that will be fun. You can make a little party out of it," Joe said.

"One step ahead of you. I invited the neighbors as well," Devin answered.

"Are they spending the night too?" Joe asked confusingly.

Devin said, "No, no. They are coming over for drinks and will meet Uncle Bill and Uncle Pete. They can stay in their own house."

"Gotcha!" Joe laughed. "Well, I know we are two thousand miles away, but if you need anything, let us know."

Devin laughed back and said, "Ok, that sounds good. We will keep you posted." Devin looked at his phone and saw that another call was coming in. It was Pat calling through.

"Your brother is calling through," Devin told Joe.

Joe laughed again and said, "Yeah, I know; he is sitting across the office from me and is messing around. I'll let you talk to him. I love you, Dad. Tell Emily I said hi, and I love her."

"Will do, buddy." Devin said goodbye and immediately clicked over to talk to Pat. As soon as Devin answered, Pat said, "That guy never stops talking!" Knowing full well that Joe was across the office from him, hearing every word.

Devin said, "Well, hello there, other son. Your brother tells me you're cracking the whip."

Pat chimed in and said, "Well, it is Vegas, and there are a lot of whips available. What happens in Vegas stays in Vegas."

Pat was never short on jokes or witty comebacks. His performing background always shone through and would always light up a room when he walked in. He still performed some stand-up comedy on the side but was so busy with his company that he didn't always have time to hit the stage. Devin and Emily always thought that between Pat and Joe, their incredible talents could have them running a movie studio.

Pat quickly turned his attention to the storm and asked all the same questions Joe had asked. Devin filled him in and continued to catch up on life in general. Towards the end of the call, Pat asked, "Did you check in with Tom? Are they hunkering down too?"

Devin knew he wanted to check in with him today and would touch base to see if they needed anything.

Devin couldn't resist and quipped back at Pat, "Hunkering, huh? That word is used every time a storm is coming. I never understood it! I never thought I would hear you use it!"

Pat laughed at his father. "True! I just thought it was still a Florida thing."

"Oh, it is," Devin replied. "Weatherman here says it every time he updates the forecast!"

Devin continued, "Anyway, the answer to your question is that I haven't talked to Tom yet but will touch base with him today.

Devin knew it was time to get off the phone. He still needed to call Tom and check on Bill to see where he was on his travels. He said goodbye to Pat, told him he loved him and ended the call.

Devin hit the contact info for Tom, and the phone began to ring.

They were grateful. Tom, Nicole, and Levi lived close, and Sunday dinners with them were always the highlight of their week. Tom worked as a parks and recreation supervisor and had worked his way up through the ranks. The local town where he lived and worked appreciated his contributions and ultimately relied on him for everything. He had a good head on his shoulders, got what he wanted out of life, and never let anyone take advantage of him. Tom was not into entertainment like his brothers, but that was a good thing since it wasn't his passion. Tom was happy spending time at home with his family, watching football on the weekends, or spending a couple of hours at the gun range. Not only did his employer rely on him, but the family did too. Everyone wanted Tom on their side because he was their protector. Sometimes gruff on the outside but a heart of gold on the inside. The phone rang on its last ring as it went to voicemail. Devin let the greeting play, and when the sound of the beep alerted him, he said, "Hey, it's your father. Just checking in. Are you at the store? Are you getting ready for the storm? Are you preparing to be hunkering for a few days? Call me when you get this. I love you." Devin hung up, went into the house, and saw Emily had the forecast on the TV. He paused as he walked by and heard the weatherman announce, "Get ready, folks. We will need to do some hunkering down with this storm."

Marisol woke up early that day after tossing and turning all night. Her new job started today, and it was all she could think about. She had rehearsed the route to her new employment at Guantanamo Bay three times and had it down to the minute she would arrive each day. Even though the forecast had Irma approaching soon, businesses and government offices would open for at least part of the day and would make a decision later on closings. Cuba had seen its share of storms, and nothing shut down too early ahead of them. They knew how to maneuver and function, and no storm really stopped the day-to-day functions for too long. Marisol, after getting dressed, made her way to the kitchen for a quick breakfast and to grab the lunch her mother had prepared for her the night before. Being the planner that she was, she made sure she allotted time for breakfast. She performed a last-minute check in the hallway mirror, adjusted her ID badge proudly displayed on her blouse, and then began her short walk to the taxi.

Marisol's mother was always an early riser and was in the kitchen to wish her luck on her first day of work. Marisol retrieved her lunch, and as she did, her mother said, "Estoy muy orgullosa de ti, dulce hija" (I am so proud of you, my sweet daughter).

Marisol hugged her mother, thanked her, and opened the door. A strong gust of wind caught the door and threw it open as it slammed against the modest house. Marisol knew it might be a little gusty and a bit rainy that morning, and of course she planned for that as well. She packed an umbrella, a raincoat, and a rain hat. She said one last goodbye to her mother, and off she went to her taxi.

Marisol was proud of herself as well. She had worked hard to get this job. She was ready to show everyone at the Navy Supply Systems Command that she was absolutely the right choice for a new hire. Before she realized it, she arrived at the taxi stand and jumped in a car that was waiting.

"Buenos días, Marisol," the taxi driver cheerfully said. He knew Marisol from the pre-planning she had done, testing taxi rides and bus journeys to Guantanamo. Marisol returned the greeting with a smile on her face. She was beyond excited and chuckled inside, pretending she was some dignitary that was just picked up by her chauffeur.

The taxi driver continued the conversation. "So, this is the big day! No more rehearsals. First day on the job!"

Marisol said, "Yes, it is!" It was all she could get out before she felt the car shift violently from a gust of wind.

The taxi driver clutched the wheel and immediately said, "Sorry about that. We are getting some gusts from Irma, and they can be a little crazy."

"Not your fault," Marisol said graciously. She looked out of the window, and before she knew it, she had arrived at the bus station. She smiled at the driver and paid him as he wished her good luck. She stepped out of the car and walked to the bus for her final leg of her journey to work.

The bus was not crowded as Marisol made her way to a seat. She looked around and only saw a few other fellow commuters. This time, she did not get one of the other bus drivers she had in the past during her test runs. She found a seat not too far back and made herself comfortable. This was a bit longer than the taxi ride, and once the bus arrived, it would drop her directly in front of the Navy Command Center. All part of her grand plan.

Marisol glanced at her watch and knew the bus was about to depart. Just as she looked up from her watch, the bus doors closed, and the driver started the loud engine and started down the road. Marisol thought for a moment that she could rest her eyes. The trip would take about thirty minutes, and she knew she would have time. Her excitement wouldn't allow her to rest. She continued to look out of the window and saw the familiar scenery. As the bus wound its way through the mountainous terrain, occasionally, she caught a glance at the sea. It was churning, and she could see some of the waves crash high over the rocks. The bus driver, she could tell, was also fighting some wind gusts but managed to do a good job of steadying the bus. As they approached another curve, Marisol saw the abandoned apartment building she had seen so many times. The building hugged the curvy road, and on the other side, it clung to the side of the mountain. She was again amazed at the engineering of the building and often thought it was abandoned because of how precariously it sat on the hill. As soon as that thought went through her head, a large gust of wind shook the bus, and it seemed to rock back and forth until finally settling. The other passengers all looked at one another for comfort when a deafening crash came from in front of the bus.

The driver practically jumped out of his seat. When Marisol looked, she saw that one of the balconies that was apparently barely clinging to the abandoned apartment building had come crashing down, blocking the roadway.

The bus driver, not missing a beat and visibly shaken said, "Ok, folks, that was close. It's too dangerous to stay here. We need to get off the bus and find some shelter until we figure out our next move."

Marisol gathered her things and began to exit the bus with the other passengers. She saw the debris in front of the bus. It was a combination of cement and wrought iron railing sprawled all over the road. The driver was leading them off to the side of the road to a vegetable stand that had been closed for quite some time but offered a little bit of shelter. All Marisol could think of was getting to her job on time for her first day. She hoped that the road could be cleared quickly or that she could find a sympathetic driver in a car nearby to take her the rest of the way.

The driver and other passengers were a few steps ahead of Marisol when another gust of wind came alive. Another crash was heard as the passengers all stared and looked again. This time, they were all looking at Marisol. Marisol was confused as she realized a few seconds had gone by. Did she black out? Why were they all looking at her? She then realized she could barely move. She felt a warm liquid dripping on her. She could *barely lift her hand to her face, and when she did, she saw blood. As she looked around her, she saw she had become one with another rusty, decaying balcony that had come to rest on top of her. Her entire body was riddled with pain she had never felt before. She saw her bag with her lunch that her mother had packed and spilled everywhere. Her company badge had come off and was floating in a puddle nearby. Her breathing was becoming shallow. She wasn't going to make her first day on the job. She looked up again and knew why no one was running to save her. It was too late. Marisol, the dreamer and the planner, slowly closed her eyes. Irma had other plans for her.*

CHAPTER 10

ARRIVAL

Emily was in full nesting mode as she prepared the house for their upcoming guests. The weather channel played in the background as she prepped some meals in the kitchen for the next few days. Dude seemed restless, which wasn't out of the ordinary when a storm was approaching. He could always sense it and would follow Devin and Emily into every room, trying to settle down and find a safe haven.

Garrett was in the living room, chatting away on his walkie-talkie with Zack. Schools had closed a day early to allow families to prepare for the arrival of the storm, and the school districts needed the schools available for possible shelters. Emily took a personal day and was happy to be home. She finished up her meal prep and decided to vacuum downstairs. The guest bedroom and bathroom were all cleaned for Bill and Pete. Emily even set up an extra dog bed in there for Bella. She knew Devin was in the shower, and Garrett was preoccupied with his instant communication with Zack on the 'Irma Central' chat line.

Emily would have to deal with Dude as she fired up the vacuum. Besides storms, like any dog cliche, he hated the vacuum. She felt bad; she was about to add to his stress, but it was the last thing she needed to do before Devin's brother arrived.

Emily began her normal route to run the hoover as she started in the living room. Garrett saw her getting closer to him in the living room and immediately yelled, "MOM!"

Emily heard his scream and turned off the vacuum.

"What?"

Garrett calmly said, 'Do you have to do that now? I'm talking to Zack."

Emily was not having it and said, "Well, unless you would like to do this, then I suggest you not have an opinion on it right now."

Garrett, sensing her annoyance, tried to change the subject. "That's not what I meant. I mean, uh, can I go to Zack's?"

Emily quickly said, "Not a chance! They are calling for everyone to be in place by this evening, and you are not going anywhere. Your uncles will be here soon, and Mr. Alan and Mr. Jack are coming over tonight for a bit as well. If you want to talk to Zack, you can go upstairs in your room and do it."

Garrett sighed heavily and talked into the walkie-talkie as he climbed the stairs to his room. "Stand by Zack One. Irma Central is moving locations."

Emily chuckled to herself as she continued vacuuming.

She glided through the downstairs easily and had one last corner to get to when she felt a hand on her shoulder.

Emily jumped and screamed in one swoop. When she came to rest on her feet, she turned to see Devin.

"What the hell?' She gasped.

Devin's response was always laughter, followed by genuine astonishment that she was scared so easily.

"I was just going to tell you Bill must have called when I was in the shower. He left a message and said they would be here in about two hours. Traffic is heavy, but they are just dealing with it."

Emily said, "Oh, good. I'm glad they will be here soon. The house is all set. I even got the guest room ready."

Devin appreciated all the thought and care that Emily put into her family. She never wavered and loved taking care of people selflessly. Devin pulled Emily close, kissed her, and said, "Thank you." He followed up with a big hug and told her, "Oh, by the way, Bill said they already stopped at the liquor store and bought ingredients for Cosmos."

Emily laughed and said, "You called that one!"

Devin laughed and continued into the bedroom to finish getting ready. Emily was able to finally finish vacuuming and put the vacuum away in the closet.

Emily was exhausted but was glad everything was ready. The house was cleaned. Food was prepped. Beds were made. Flashlights had batteries. Ice bags were filled.

Devin walked into the kitchen and saw that Emily needed to sit and chill for a few minutes. He turned to her and said, "Let's grab a couple of beers and sit by the pool before we have our house guests."

Emily didn't hesitate and said, "Sounds good."

They maneuvered around the wall of outdoor furniture by the sliding glass door and went outside by the pool. Devin opened the little pool refrigerator and grabbed two beers. He quickly realized after the storm prep that all the pool chairs were inside. He was about to go inside and drag two chairs out when he saw Emily already sitting on the edge of the pool with her shoes off and her feet dangling in the water. He changed direction and walked over to join her. Fortunately, Devin never put shoes on after his shower and sat down next to her. He handed her a beer as they clinked the cans together and enjoyed the first cold, crisp sip.

"Are you ready for Bill and Pete and Bella and Alan and Jack and the baby?" Devin asked.

Emily responded. "Your brother and Pete, their dog, and your neighbors are the least of my worries. I'm just hoping the storm isn't bad and Garrett and Dude don't get too anxious."

Devin went into comfort mode and said, "They will be fine, and we will manage through the storm. We always do. We will have a fun night, have a few drinks to relax, hear some fun stories from my brother, and before you know it, it will be morning."

Emily smiled and relished in the moment. She tilted her head up towards the sun to soak it in, then said, "It's so strange that a hurricane is approaching. Other than a little wind right now, it's pleasant. No one would ever guess we are waiting for the arrival of a major storm. It's relatively calm."

Devin took a long sip of his beer and said, "Let's hope it stays that way."

CHAPTER 11

HOUSEGUESTS

The doorbell rang, and the house sprang to life. Dude began barking, Garrett came running down the stairs, still shouting at Zack on the other end of his new toy, and Alexa sprang to life, sharing the latest storm update. Devin and Emily were in the living room watching TV as the simultaneous commotion unraveled. Devin silenced Alexa as they both headed towards the door. Garrett knew his uncles were here, but he was most excited about Bella. He loved it when Bella and Dude played together, and he happily took on his own doggie daycare in his room.

Devin opened the door, as Dude was anxious to get outside. He heard and smelled Bella, and he was crying to get to her. As he opened the door, there was Bella wagging her tail and barking at Dude as he greeted her. Garrett ran out as well and said, "Look who it is, boy! It's Bella. She's spending the night with us." They ran to the front yard and immediately began playing. Emily and Devin saw Bill and Pete near their car as they began to unload.

Bill looked up and saw Devin and said, "Hi, baby brother." Devin said, "Well, hello there, travelers." He gave Bill a hug, made his way over to Pete, and did the same.

Pete jokingly said, "Well, I guess I will take a hug from you first."

Emily walked to Pete and said, "Saving the best for last, I see." She gave Pete a warm hug and said, "Welcome, you two." She went right over to Bill and gave him a hug as well.

Devin said, "Let us help you get everything inside."

"That would be great," Bill said.

"What a horrific drive that was!" Pete jumped in.

"I can imagine," Emily said. "We have been watching the news and seeing all the evacuations down south. The roads have to be insane."

"That's an understatement," Bill replied. "I think we got out just in time."

Devin gathered a suitcase and tucked a cooler under his arm. Emily grabbed a small bag as they all headed towards the front door. Garrett, Dude, and Bella were all rolling around on the grass. Emily said to Garrett, "Come say hi to your uncles."

"We know Bella rates higher than we do!" Pete said.

"Sorry, Uncle Bill. Sorry, Uncle Pete," Garrett said as he walked over to say hi and give them an awkward hug with their hands full of bags.

As they stood briefly on the front porch, they all noticed that the skies that seemed clear just a few moments ago had become gray and the wind had suddenly picked up.

"We were driving through some squalls on the way here. It looks like it's catching up to us," Bill said.

They all headed inside, and Garrett made sure Bella and Dude were safely inside as well.

Emily walked Bill and Pete directly to the guest room. They were lucky that the guest room and private bathroom were on the first floor. Devin and Emily's room was off the kitchen on the other side of the house. There were two bedrooms and a loft upstairs for Patty and Garrett, so when they had houseguests, everyone had their own private space.

Bill and Pete immediately saw the little dog bed Emily had set up for Bella.

"Oh my god, you are so sweet," Bill said to Emily.

Emily smiled and said, "Of course, Bella must have her own bed. I know she is like Dude and will probably end up in bed with you, but it's there if she wants it." Just as she said that Bella and Dude came busting into the room as if Dude were showing Bella where she was staying.

"Well, let me say hi to you, Dude," Pete said, giving him a warm pat on the head and a quick rub down. "Thank you for letting Bella sleep over with you."

Bella and Dude ran around the room and quickly ran out again. They heard Garrett say, "Come on, you two, let's go up to my room." The thunder of paws and feet was heard running up the stairs.

Devin, by this point, had joined them in the room and dropped a bag down. Emily said, "Ok, you both know the routine. Make yourself at home. Help yourself to whatever you want."

Bill said, "Thank you so much. I just need to find a spot for these few groceries we bought." He held up a couple of bags to show them.

Pete laughed and said, "Yes, our groceries." He mimed air quotes. "It's all the ingredients for Cosmos."

Bill said, "You will grocery your way; I will grocery mine."

They all laughed, and Emily said, "Let me put this away. You guys get settled in. We are having our neighbors over at around 6:30 just for some hors d'oeuvres and drinks. A mini hurricane party."

Pete lit up and said, "Yes, Devin told us! Sounds fun. I can't wait to meet them."

"You will love them," Emily answered. "Oh, and I am so glad you decided to come here. It makes me feel better."

Bill and Pete smiled as she shut the door and let them freshen up.

Devin and Emily headed to the kitchen to unpack the grocery bags. Emily looked at the clock, and it was five fifteen. She knew Alan, Jack, and Sloan would be there in about an hour. She had a few things she had to put in the oven, so she started the prep work for the few finger foods that needed heating up.

Emily turned to Devin and said, "Do you think we have enough food?"

Devin replied, "Yes, plenty. You always worry, and there is always enough."

"I feel bad; it's not really dinner. It's all finger food." Emily said.

"We are hosting a small little hurricane gathering with drinks and snacks. Don't overthink it." Devin said.

"I guess you're right," she replied.

Devin looked at the counter after they unpacked Bill and Pete's grocery bags. "Well, we certainly have enough booze."

Emily laughed and said, "Yes, enough for the whole hurricane season!"

A few minutes passed, and Pete and Bill walked into the kitchen and cheerfully said,

"Did someone mention booze?"

Devin said, "Yes, we were just commenting on how well prepared you came."

Pete said, "We don't leave home without it. Ok, Bill, do your magic and make a batch."

Bill was already on it and began to stage all the ingredients he needed for a batch of cosmos. Emily knew it would be about another forty-five minutes until the neighbors arrived and joined in.

"I'm not ready for one yet but go ahead and make a batch. Bill, you have to work around me. I just need to get some of the food ready."

Bill replied, "Pretend I'm not even here" as he began the orchestration of his famous concoction. A cosmopolitan was Bill and Pete's drink of choice. A combination of vodka, cranberry juice, lime, and triple sec. A simple enough drink but with a powerful punch.

Emily placed the snacks and a nice charcuterie tray on the kitchen counter. Always worried about not having enough food, earlier she made a batch of her famous meatballs and had them cooking in the crock pot.

Every time they had a gathering, guests would always end up in the kitchen. Emily had decorated the house perfectly and took everything into consideration. A large table accommodated all the family when they came over. The big kitchen island sat even more people, and a tastefully placed sofa in the corner by a window would allow more family to sit and, most of the time, watch Emily do her magic in the kitchen. With Patty at school, the boys were grown and out of the house, and Garrett often hung out with his friends. Most of the time, Dude would take ownership of the little couch in the corner. Patty often deemed it the coffee couch. Whenever she was home, she sipped her morning coffee and cuddled with Dude on it.

Pete came in from the guest room and complimented Emily on the house. "You do such a nice job decorating. I think you missed your calling."

"I will leave that to the professionals. I just do it for fun and to see what suits us," she responded.

Devin was sitting at the counter as Bill and Emily danced around each other in the kitchen. Bill finished up his mixology session and started pouring it into glasses.

"Ok, who is drinking?" Bill asked.

Devin looked at the clock, and it was just about six fifteen. He would indulge in a small one, but it was a bit too early in the evening to start throwing them back. He also wanted to keep his wits about him as the storm was beginning to approach. If anything should happen, he wanted to be aware and prepared. He also knew Alan, Jack, and the baby were stopping by soon and would save a couple of drinks to have with them too.

"Well, you didn't waste any time, did you, love?" Pete chimed in.

Bill immediately said, "Is this a hurricane party or not?"

Devin said, "Pour me a small one for now. I need to get some food in me before we start drinking."

Emily said, "I'm good for now. I might have a glass of wine in a bit."

Bill poured three large drinks, ignoring Devin's request for a small one. Devin didn't argue and knew he would just nurse that one. He saw the pitcher of drinks that Bill had made and noticed how large it was. Emily gave him one of the large water pitchers they use at dinner sometimes. This time, it was filled with cosmos. He also noticed the large bottle of vodka Bill and Pete had brought with them. It was the largest you could purchase, and after Bill made the first batch, it still looked like it had a lot left in it. After Pete held his glass up, indicating a toast was about to be made, everyone else followed suit. Emily held up the water bottle she had next to her. Pete announced, "To our hosts for this Hurricane Irma gathering; We love you and thank you for letting us hunker down here."

Devin said, "There is no need to thank us. It's what family does."

No sooner did Devin complete that thought when the doorbell rang again. Bella and Dude came tearing down the stairs from Garrett's room, barking loudly as if they had never heard a doorbell before. Garrett came racing down right after them and went right to the door. Devin had just arrived at the front door and was holding the dogs back. They were both wagging their tails and were excited to see who the next visitor might be. There was no window or peep hole on the door, but he knew it must have been Alan, Jack, and Sloan. Devin opened the door and saw Alan and Jack. Jack was holding Sloan, and Alan had a diaper bag and a large bottle of wine.

"Hello neighbors," Devin greeted them. "Welcome to Irma Central," he said, glancing at Garrett with a smile, knowing he would appreciate him using the term he deemed appropriate for his communication with Zack. The dogs raced outside to the grass again, and Garrett chased after them, quickly saying hi to Alan and Jack as they entered the house.

Devin yelled to Garrett, "Bring them in, Garrett. It's very windy and starting to rain."

Alan said to Devin, "We come bearing gifts," as he handed him the bottle of wine.

"It won't go with those cookies I made for you. Only a good glass of milk for those." Jack said awkwardly.

Devin politely chuckled then said," Completely unnecessary for the wine but thank you. Come on in. Everyone is in the kitchen." Devin saw Jack holding Sloan and said, "Hi there Sloan? How are you sweetie?" Devin knew he wasn't waiting for a nine-month-old to answer and they headed toward the kitchen.

Emily saw Alan and Jack and gave them her usual warm greeting and hugs. She then without missing beat took Sloan from Jack and said, "Hello sweet girl."

Emily needed her baby fix and would take advantage anytime the neighbors were over, or they went to their house.

Devin began the introductions as Bill and Pete stood up. "Bill and Pete, these are our incredible neighbors, Alan and Jack."

Bill responded and said, "We have heard so much about you. It's nice to finally meet you."

Bill said, "You too. Devin and Emily talk about you two all the time."

Jack jumped in and joked, "We had a baby with us when we came in" He looked and saw Emily out on the back porch holding Sloan and talking with her as she showed her the pool and some birds that landed on the fence.

"That's our baby, Sloan" Jack said pointing outside.

"It was" Devin said. "I think she is Emily's now."

Bill saw the drinks on the counter and broke the ice and said, "Well looks like you started without us."

Pete loved the snarky comment and replied, "Well you will just have to catch up."

Bill heading this grabbed two more glasses and poured the new guests some drinks.

Jack said, "Let me guess, Cosmos?"
Pete said, "Oh are you a fan of these?"
Alan laughed and said, "Aren't all gays?"

That was enough to keep the icebreaking momentum going as they heard the wind pick up outside. Emily came racing back inside with Sloan, just as they heard the front door slam at the same time. Garrett came back in with the dogs and ran back upstairs with them.

Emily turned to everyone and said, "Well it cleared for two minutes then seems like a small rain band just came through. The weather is taking a turn for the worst." Just as she finished saying that Alexa obviously listening in announced, "Would you like to hear the latest weather report regarding Hurricane Irma?"

Normally Emily would reject Alexa but seeing how the wind and rain were starting to pick up she replied, "Yes"
Alexa seemed almost eerily happy to regale them with the latest report. "Hurricane Irma has just passed over the Florida Keys with sustained winds of one hundred and thirty five miles per hour and is expected to continue a northern

turn over the state throughout the evening before passing over Marco Island and southern most counties. Expect strong rain bands and heavy wind with sustained winds of over one hundred miles per hour with stronger gusts occasionally."

Everyone had stopped to hear the ominous computerized announcement. Emily looked at Devin with a look of worry and said, "Maybe we should turn on the news."

Bill breaking the ice said, "Well good thing we got out of town when we did."

Pete said, "Oh I hope the house is ok."

Alan sipped on his drink and said, "Oh right. We heard you built a house down near Naples?"

Jack responded and said, "We love it down there."

Bill glanced at Jack and said, "Let us know next time you are down. We will show you the house."

Pete looked at Bill as he heard the flirtatious tone and said, "You'll have to forgive my husband. He is a shameless flirt."
"Oh stop" Bill said laughing. "I'm just trying to be neighborly."
Pete said, "Well they are Devin and Emily's neighbors, not ours" They all shared a laugh then Bill decided it was time for drink refills.

"Who is ready for another?" Bill sung out.

Everyone's hand went up except for Devin and Emily. Devin was still nursing his drink and Emily was content with her water.

Bill said, "Come on Devin. You're falling behind."

Devin politely said, "No I'm good. Just pacing myself."

Devin knew he was only having one drink. He saw the worry on Emily's face after hearing Alexa's update. Not only that, but he also didn't feel comfortable drinking heavily with a major storm approaching. He knew Garrett would be scared and didn't want to be inebriated if he needed to react to anything that might happen.

As Alan and Jack and Bill and Pete continued to talk and get aquatinted, Emily dug through Sloan's diaper bag. They always came fully prepared, and she took out a little play mat and a few toys and sat her down in the kitchen rug by the sofa. Emily gave Devin a tilt of her head indicating she wanted to talk privately in the other room.

Devin picked up the signal right away as they walked into the living room. Emily immediately turned on the tv and she set it right to the weather channel.

"Ok I'm a little worried. Seems like Irma is getting stronger. I know the southern coast is getting hit hard but it looks like we will really get hit tonight." Emily said nervously.

Devin went into protection mode and said, "We have been through these before. It's going to be ok."

As he hugged Emily, Bill popped his head around the corner and said, "New batch!' As he held up the newly filled pitcher of cosmos. Emily pulled from Devin's embrace and said, "Go ahead and pour without us. By the way, there is plenty of food on the counter, everyone eats something."

Bill chuckled and joked, "This is my dinner" showing her the pitcher.

Bill went back into the kitchen and Devin apologetically smiled at Emily for his brother's behavior and said "Houseguests" and shrugged his shoulder. Just then the lights flickered, and the television cut out then came back on. Then all the cell phones in the house went off at once blaring the emergency broadcast siren.

CHAPTER 12

EFFECTS

Devin and Emily heard the thunderous sound of footsteps as Garrett and the two dogs came racing down the stairs. Garrett ran up to his parents, still standing in the living room, looking at their phones and reading the weather warning.

Garrett said nervously, "Did you see the lights flicker? My computer turned on and off, and then my phone went crazy." He was retelling the story as if the occurrences only happened to him in his room.

Devin said, "Yes, buddy, it's okay. Lights are on; everything is working." Emily chimed in and said, "Why don't you run upstairs and grab your iPad and anything else you want to bring down and hang out in our room?"

Garrett didn't need to be asked twice, and he ran back up the stairs. Emily would feel better if he was downstairs with them, especially if the storm was getting worse. They went back to looking at their phones and saw the emergency alert that read, 'IRMA NOW A MAJOR HURRICANE AND HEADING

NORTH THROUGH THE INTERIOR OF FLORIDA PENINSULA. POWER OUTAGES AND STRONG DAMAGING WINDS ARE LIKELY. FLOODING IN LOW-LYING AREAS IS CERTAIN. TORNADO WATCH IN EFFECT THROUGH 7:00 a.m. EST. SEEK SHELTER AND STAY IN PLACE.'

Just as they both finished reading the ominous message, they heard laughter coming from the kitchen. The effects of the alcohol that was flowing freely in the other room was obvious. Jack popped his head around the corner and said, "Well, that was a scary message. Come on you two, come take your mind off the storm and drink with us."

Devin and Emily were not really in the mood and wanted to keep their due diligence and focus on Irma, who was quickly heading towards them. The first bands were hitting them, and they knew Garrett and Dude were going to need their attention. Devin responded to Jack's request and said, "We will be in. Just getting Garrett settled."

"Okay," Jack sang. "Not too much longer. We are beginning to think you don't like us."

"Oh, stop," Emily spoke lightly, trying not to show her nervousness. "We will be right in."

Garrett had returned with his favorite pillow, a blanket, his iPad, and a backpack full of random things that he thought he might need to settle in downstairs for the night.

Emily turned to him and said, "Why don't you put your things in our room, then go eat something before it gets too late? Devin saw that it was already seven thirty and was getting hungry himself. He said to Emily, "We should get back into the kitchen."

They walked back into the kitchen as they saw Bill mixing yet another batch of drinks. Bill saw them and said, "Well, there you two are."

"I think they snuck off for a quickie," Pete slurred.

Emily shot him a look, hoping that Garrett didn't hear his comment. He hadn't, as he was still in their room setting up camp.

Bill jumped in and yelled, "Pete, stop that!"

Devin, feeling the need to change the subject, said, "It looks like it's going to be bad tonight. Everyone read the weather alert?"

Alan said, "I am so glad we are safe. We can't thank you enough for hosting this tonight." He clanged Bill's glass and noticed he was running low. Bill saw the near-empty glass and said, "You need a refill."

Alan got weirdly close to Bill and said, "Yes, I do."

Emily had made her way over to Sloan, who was sound asleep on the carpet on the blanket she laid down for her.

She grabbed a throw from the couch and covered her.

Jack saw her and said, "Oh, thank you, Emily. I almost forgot she was there."

Emily shook it off but thought it was a strange comment. It wasn't shocking that Jack would say something a little off, but that comment hit her the wrong way. They were all drinking heavily, and she noticed the very large bottle of vodka was already halfway gone. The counter looked like a mixology war zone. She noticed they had eaten some of the food, but there was still plenty left. Garrett came back in and began to make himself a plate. Bill saw him and said, "There's our little nephew. How's it going, Garrett? How's school? Any girlfriends?"

Garrett sheepishly shook his head. Pete decided to weigh in and said, "What about a boyfriend?"

Emily felt the need to jump in this time, and her tone was not masked, and she said, "Come on, Pete."

Devin and Emily were far from homophobic but there was a time and place for everything. This was not that time.

Emily helped Garrett with his plate and told him he could eat in their room. She knew he had some shows downloaded on his iPad to keep him occupied. He was also still communicating with Zack on his walkie-talkie. Garrett happily headed into the bedroom.

Devin's phone rang, and he looked down and saw it was Tom. He excused himself to take the call in his office, but not before glaring at Pete for his stupid comment. He passed through the living room around the corner and closed the office door behind him.

"Hey. I was hoping I would get a chance to talk to you," he said into the phone.

"Hey Dad. You guys doing, okay?" Tom asked.

"Yes, we are good. Uncle Bill and Uncle Pete are here. They decided to drive away from the coast and ride it out here. How about you? How's Nicole and Levi?" He knew his daughter-in-law and grandson were safe when it came to living with Tom. He had grown into such a great dad and husband. Devin and Emily were so proud of him and everything he had accomplished.

Tom answered, "Everyone is good. I have the whole house prepped, and we are as ready as we can be. It's getting nasty out there."

Devin said, "Yes, it's supposed to be even worse tonight. I'm glad you called back. I touched base with your brothers and Patty and just wanted to make sure you all were okay. Another roar of laughter could be heard from the kitchen, and it spilled all the way to the front of the house, where Devin's office was.

"Sounds like a party. Thanks for the invite." Tom jokingly said.

"You have no idea," Devin replied. "We invited Alan and Jack over to meet your uncles and to have a few drinks. I think they are well past a few drinks already. I'm starting to regret the invite.

Tom said, "Yeah, I talked with Pat and Joe earlier, and they said Uncle Bill and Uncle Pete would be there. Let me guess, Cosmo Fest?"

Devin laughed. Tom always had a funny sense of humor. Besides being a truly strong, rugged, no-nonsense type of guy, he was also incredibly quick-witted.

"Yes, of course." Devin said, still laughing.

Devin heard Nicole yell at Tom in the background.

"Hey Dad, Nicole needs my help with something. I have to run."

Devin said, "Of course. Family first. Please tell Nicole and Levi, we love them and stay safe."

"You too, Dad. Tell Emily and Garrett the same. Let me know if you need anything. Love you." Devin hung up the phone and smiled. Tom often ended his phone calls with, 'Let me know if you need anything'. It wasn't just rhetorical; Tom meant it. It was the type of man he had become. Devin's reflection on his proud father moment was short-lived, as he heard a huge crash from outside. He quickly went to the window and looked outside. It was dark by now, and he couldn't see anything on his site that could have made that noise. He did notice how fierce it seemed outside. There was something about this storm that made him uneasy. He opened the office door and rounded the corner to the living room. There on the floor laughing was Bill as Jack was trying to pick him up. Devin realized that the loud thud he heard wasn't from outside, but from his already inebriated brother falling to the floor. Bill and Jack didn't see Devin yet, as he saw Jack stroke Bill's face and say, "I hope you're not hurt." Bill responded and said, "I like a little pain once in a while." Devin was witnessing yet another awkward, flirtatious moment. The two were alone in the room, and the cosmos that were racing through their bloodstreams were unblocking any inhibitions.

Devin said loudly to make himself known, "Wow, I thought a tree fell on the house." Jack jumped as Bill stumbled to his feet. "Are you calling me a fat little brother?"

Devin quickly walked by them on his way to the kitchen and said in passing, "No, no. Not at all. I just thought it came from outside." Devin was glad to be away from whatever he had just witnessed. He walked into the kitchen and saw Emily sitting at the counter next to Sloan, who was still fast asleep on the floor. Emily was looking at her phone, checking on storm updates. Pete and Alan were at the other end of the counter, with freshly poured drinks and in deep conversation.

A huge rush of wind could be heard outside as the rain sounded like pellets hitting the windows. Devin was feeling uneasy, and he could only imagine how Emily was feeling.

He thought about pouring a drink but decided against it. He needed to stick to his non-participation in the spirits and keep his wits about him.

He knew the effects of the storm were going to be strong. He was also witnessing the effects of the vodka that kept flowing with the houseguests. He decided to grab some water from the refrigerator, and as he opened the door, all the lights in the house went black.

The Florida Keys have seen many storms over the years. As bad as many of them were, the keys always seemed to be mysteriously protected. Not to say that they never had damage; it just never suffered the extreme devastation that other regions suffered. The storm was intense, and most residents were locked in their homes at this point. Captain Barry was not one of them. He was locked inside his trusty 'Hook Em' and planned to ride it out. Most weekend sailors scrambled and removed their boats from their slips before a storm came. The seasoned sailors kept their boats in the water. It was where they were meant to be. Captain Barry had ridden out storms before on his boat. He had also been through monstrous, treacherous waters during his time in the Navy. He had everything he needed to weather the storm since he spent most of the time there instead of in his trailer a few miles away. Captain Barry was a simple man and was most happy when he was on his boat. He was settled in the cabin below and sitting at his table, working on his third pot of coffee. He was happily listening to the radio and skimming

through the local newspaper. He loved listening to public radio stations, especially ones that involved sailing. He was enamored by anything that involved the sea. He dialed the ancient radio and, through the static, found one of his favorite programs. The boat was rocking, and he could hear the winds howling outside. Most of the boat slips around him were empty, but a few remained occupied with boats. Luckily, the few that did remain had Captain Barry's famous improvised pump that kept the water away as best it could. He knew of one other boat captain who was riding the storm out. He was on the other side of the marina, and Captain Barry could see a light glimmering from inside the mid-size fishing boat. As the wind picked up and the boat swayed, Captain Barry wasn't fazed. He knew how to function and maneuver during storms. He even had a unique way to secure the boat so it could handle the incessant movement. To him, this was fun. A way of life. As he sat there listening to his program, he could hear an odd sound coming from the dock. It was barely audible, and he needed to turn down the radio to see if he could identify the sound. Captain Barry turned his body towards the small window below deck that was behind him. He glanced out, and although it was dark, he could see the dock illuminated by the single dock light that was near his boat slip.

He still couldn't see much as he peered through the rain that was now coming down steadily. He thought he would ignore it, but the sound was constant. A whipping sound with a distinct tinging. Captain Barry had become accustomed to the various sounds of not only the sea but of the boat dock. This was an unusual sound that needed investigating. He grabbed his rain jacket and a flashlight and headed above. He opened the latch and was faced with a gust of wind and pellets of raindrops. A few of his business cards, which he kept in a small plastic wall display just inside the latch, blew into the wind. He pushed through the beating rain and stood on deck as he shined his flashlight around. He saw the boat across from him that he helped secure before the storm hit. A local weekend sailor that Captain Barry helped installed one of his pumps He could see the pump secured on the dock and doing what it was intended to do. The pumps required power, which is usually accessed via a waterproof and weatherproof outlet box by each slip. As Captain Barry continued to shine his flashlight at the pump, he followed the extension cord to the outlet. When he did, he noticed something else plugged into the second socket. He climbed off the "Hook Em' and made his way to the outlet. When he got closer, he noticed there was a phone charger with a long cord flapping in the wind and whipping the aluminum pole that the outlet was secured to. This was the annoying sound he kept hearing. He knew some of the local kids who were hired to clean fish would use the outlets to charge their phones. It is a harmless habit, but sometimes annoying to those who pay a monthly fee to the marina and use the outlets. Some kid obviously unplugged their phone and neglected to grab the charger. Captain Barry was not going to listen to the constant pinging sound all night and decided he would unplug the charger and store it on the boat. He wasn't even sure if anyone would be missing it, as most kids probably had multiple chargers. As he grabbed the charger, he noticed how frayed the cord was. He wasn't sure if this was the original condition of the cord or what had happened to it after the wind kept thrashing it against the pole. As he grabbed the cord, he felt a shock run up his arm. He immediately cursed and threw the cord down as it bounced in the water. He was annoyed at this point after making the *effort and braving the storm for a piece of crap phone charger. At least the annoying sound would be gone, he thought as he made his way back to his boat. Still holding on to his flashlight, he walked the short distance and felt another tingle run up his arm. He looked down at his arm and realized it wasn't his right arm that he originally felt the shock before he dropped the cord. This pain was running up his left arm. He walked two more steps, then felt immense pain in his chest as he clutched it and dropped to his knees. He tried to stay upright, but before he knew it, he was face down on the dock. The flashlight fell from his hand and rolled on the dock. The pain was unbearable and immeasurable. The wind and rain were even stronger now. Captain Barry, the tough sea captain and rugged navy veteran, was becoming lifeless. He tried to fight it, then realized there was nothing he could do. No one was around to see him or get to him. The only other occupant was all the way on the other side of the marina, safely inside their boat and not hearing anything but the howling winds. Captain Barry's eyes were getting heavy as the heart attack was taking over. Before his eyes shut for the last time, he saw the flashlight that had rolled on the dock. It came to rest and magically illuminated the back of his boat. 'Hook Em' had a final spotlight for the proud captain to see as he closed his eyes. Irma was winning.*

CHAPTER 13

POUNDING

As soon as the power went out, everyone reacted with an audible yell. Devin took his phone and turned on the flashlight. He made his way over to the table in the kitchen, where he had candles and battery-operated lanterns standing by. He turned on the two lanterns he had and moved them onto the kitchen counter.

Alan, Jack, Bill, and Pete were working on another pitcher of cosmos before the lights went out. Other than their initial reaction, it barely fazed them, and when Devin illuminated the kitchen again, it was a welcome relief because now they could see to pour more drinks. Devin made his way over to Emily. She had her phone light on already, checking on Sloan, who was still fast asleep on the blanket, this time with Dude and Bella curled up next to her. She looked at Devin and said, "Can you stand here for a second? I want to check on Garrett."

Emily thought it was strange that Garrett didn't come out of the room when the house lost power. She opened the door to their bedroom and saw Garrett with headphones on and glaring at his iPad. He was completely unaware of the power outage, with the full glow of the screen illuminating his face. Emily tapped him on the shoulder. Garrett jumped a bit and took off his headphones. Emily said, "The power went out. You, ok?" Garrett looked around the room and saw that it was darker than normal and that the one nightstand light that had been on was now off.

He said to Emily," I didn't even notice. Let me check to see if Zack's lights are out." Emily knew that the whole neighborhood was probably without power, but she let Garrett enjoy his reconnaissance. She turned to Garrett and said, "We are all still in the kitchen if you need us." Garrett nodded his head and began his call to Zack on the walkie-talkie. As Emily walked out, all she heard was static coming from a small speaker on the device. Zack either didn't have his turned on or the storm was causing interference.

When Emily arrived back in the kitchen, she saw more drinks flowing, and Devin was now tending to Sloan, who was stirring on the blanket. "She just started to wake up, and she is a little fussy," Devin said to Emily. Emily looked at her two dads, who were obviously feeling no pain. They were still talking and laughing as they discussed the best parts of Liza Minelli's Nineteen Seventy's television special in detail with Bill and Pete. Emily looked at Devin and whispered, "I think Sloan is hungry. I don't think Alan or Jack are in any shape to feed her." She grabbed an empty bottle from the diaper bag and handed it to Devin. "Can you fill this up with some milk?" Devin grabbed the bottle and made his way to the refrigerator. He opened the refrigerator, grabbed the milk, and placed it on the counter. He placed the bottle down and began to fill it.

"Oh, you've resorted to milk now?" Pete quipped.

Devin wasn't in the mood for joking and just politely chuckled. "No, it's for the baby," he said.

Alan quickly jumped in and said, "Oh my gosh. Thank you, Devin. Thank you, Emily. "He was just realizing that they had been caring for Sloan as they all enjoyed the never-ending happy hour.

Emily said in her ever-gentle tone," Oh, it's fine. She has been sleeping most of the time."

Devin finished pouring the milk and screwed the top back on. He walked the bottle over to Emily and handed it to her as she began to feed Sloan. Devin looked up and saw that Jack had left the group at the end of the counter. Alan and Bill had moved on to the best Broadway musicals and were deep in discussion. Pete was picking at some food as he sipped yet another drink. Devin was curious to see where Jack had gone too. He probably went to use the bathroom, but Devin wanted to be sure. He grabbed some more battery-powered candles along with another lantern. He walked into the very dark living room and looked to his left at the small hallway where the bathroom was. The door was open, but since there was no power, it was hard to tell if someone was in there. He placed a few lit candles on the coffee table, then took the lantern and peered around the corner into the bathroom. He held the lantern up and jumped back as he saw his own reflection in the mirror. He was glad Emily didn't see that after all the teasing he had given her for being so jumpy. He walked back into the living room and looked around. Maybe he walked right by Jack, and he was sitting on the couch. Devin investigated more and discovered the couch was empty. Just then, he heard a slight pounding. The storm was orchestrating various sounds outside, but this was coming from inside. Devin stopped to get his bearings in the dark room. The sound wasn't overly loud and was close by. He held up the lantern and realized the pounding was coming from the foyer. He walked slowly to that area and rounded the corner carefully. He held up the light and saw Jack. He was pacing like a caged animal. Devin stood there for a moment and saw that, since it was so dark, Jack was drunkenly walking into the walls. Like a wind-up toy, he was walking back and forth. When a wall stopped him, he turned around and walked towards the other one. Devin wanted to get his attention and called out his name, "Jack?" He got no response and tried again. "Jack?"

As if freed from a trance, he looked up at Devin. It was an eerie sight, as his eyes were bloodshot and glazed and seemed to glow in the darkness. Jack mumbled something incoherent and then seemed to make a gesture towards his zipper. Devin panicked and thought Jack was going to relieve himself right in the front hallway. He got closer to Jack and said, "Jack, are you okay?" Jack spun around and said some gibberish about milk and cookies. Devin couldn't figure out what he was trying to say. Maybe he was making another reference to the cookies he delivered before. He grabbed Jack and said, "Jack, do you need to go to the bathroom?" This time, Jack just stared at Devin. He leaned on the wall and slowly started pounding it with his fist. It wasn't a violent pounding but a slow, methodical thump.

Devin had socialized with Alan and Jack many times, but he never witnessed Jack in this state. Something was off. It was more than just an abundance of alcohol. It was almost as if Jack was possessed. It was a ridiculous notion, but it was the only way he could describe what was happening.

Devin made sure Jack was safely leaning against the wall. A huge gust of wind could be heard outside as the whole house seemed to rattle. Devin heard more pounding but realized this time it was his heartbeat. It was time to end this little weird hurricane gathering, he thought, as he went to get Alan.

CHAPTER 14

GOODNIGHT

Devin made his way back to the kitchen, got Alan's attention, and asked, "Can I talk to you for a second?"

Pete, always feeling the need to add a comment, said, "Oh Devin, are you stealing him away from me?" Devin ignored the comment completely.

"Is everything okay, Devin?" Emily asked.

Devin, not wanting to draw too much attention to the situation, responded and said, "Yes, all good."

Still holding the lantern, he guided Alan past the living room and brought him directly to Jack. Jack was now turned around and facing them. Even though Devin had seen him before, it was still somewhat scary to see his neighbor in that demonic state. Alan was feeling no pain at this point and could barely process what was going on. Devin then said, "I think you should get him home. It's pretty bad outside, but I will help you gather everything and walk you next door." Alan nodded as Devin truly hoped he understood.

Alan and Jack's house was only about twenty steps away, and with Devin's help, they could easily make it safely. The site of Jack seemed to sober Alan up enough to agree that they needed to leave. Bill heard the commotion and had joined them in the foyer. "Is everything okay?" he said, slurring his words. Devin turned to his brother and said, "Yes, fine. We need to get Jack home." Jack, at this point, was talking incoherently, as if he were speaking in tongues. Bill, not sensing anything was wrong and oblivious to the situation, began talking to Jack.

"It was so nice to meet you both. We really must stay in touch," Devin said to Bill. "Stay here with Jack." He left, knowing that he couldn't leave the both of them for long.

As he passed through the living room, heading back into the kitchen, he noticed the clock in the glow of the candles. It was ten o'clock. It's time to wrap up this night, he thought. He walked into the kitchen and said to Emily, "Alan and Jack are heading home."

She sensed the urgency in his voice and picked up Sloan, gathered her things, and placed them in the diaper bag. Alan walked in and was trying his best to hold it together, like a drunk driver trying to convince the police officer who pulled him over that he wasn't drinking. He stabilized himself on the counter and began to say his goodbyes. Pete was still sitting at the counter and was in no shape to stand up, but he managed to spit out a sloppy goodbye. He said to Alan in another oddly provocative tone, "It was so nice to meet you. Please, let's get together again." Alan was only half listening as he grabbed the diaper bag from Emily. Devin grabbed Sloan and carried her to the foyer as Emily followed. As they made their way to the foyer, Jack was incoherently talking in circles. Bill was just leaning on the wall, holding himself up, smiling, and nodding his head.

Emily turned to Devin, and before she could say anything, he said quietly, "I'm walking them home. It has to be quick because it's pretty bad out there." Emily said, "Wait, let me grab a jacket to put around Sloan.' She ran to the guest room closet and grabbed an older windbreaker that they barely used anymore. By this time, Pete had stumbled from the kitchen as everyone was now gathered in the foyer.

Devin thought he just needed to get his neighbors home and get his brother and Pete to bed. Emily arrived back with the jacket and wrapped it around Sloan in hopes of protecting her from the driving rain. Sloan was pretty content, considering everything that was going on.

Devin turned to Bill and said, "Emily's going to open the door, and we need to try and do this quickly." He knew Alan was only comprehending some of the orders that were being barked at him, but it would have to do. He looked at Jack and said, "Jack, we have to make this quick and get you home." Jack let out an odd giggle. Devin still didn't understand what was going on with Jack, and at that point, he didn't care. He wanted them home.

He looked at Alan, who had the diaper bag, and Jack, who seemed to be in another world but was briefly coherent enough to understand that once the door opened, there was no turning back. Emily said to Devin, "Are you ready?" Devin nodded his head as he got close to the door. It was still going to be difficult with their annoying door that opened outward, but it was time to do it. Emily opened the door as the wind relentlessly howled and made its way into the house. The porch roof was doing nothing to protect them from the rain that was now sideways and pelting the house. Devin ran off the porch into the storm as Alan and Jack followed. Devin had made it to their porch in no time and looked back to see if Alan and Jack were behind him. They weren't moving as fast, but somehow, they made it to the porch. Jack still seemed dazed and confused. The pelting rain seemed to have sobered Alan up enough for him to grab the house keys and quickly unlock the door. Devin handed Sloan to Alan and guided Jack inside the house. Alan tried to thank Devin, but he was already gone, running back to his porch. Devin landed back on his porch and briefly looked out at the street. He could barely tell it was his neighborhood. The street was completely black. He could make out the glow of flashlights and candles from some of the other neighbors, houses, but there was a deadness to the street. He quickly opened the door, where he saw Emily waiting with a towel. Devin was drenched and dried off the best he could. Bill and Pete had made their way to the living room and were sitting on the couch. Pete's head was nodding back as if he were going to pass out in a second. Bill was trying to say what a fun night it had been with Alan and Jack, but nothing coming out of his mouth was making sense. Emily turned to Devin and said, "I'm going to check on Garrett." As she left, she looked at Devin again and gave him a look. He knew, after years of marriage, what the look was. He needed to get his brother and Pete to bed. Devin was at his wits end at this point and wasn't mincing words. "Ok, you two. We are beat and are going to see if we can rest at all tonight. Emily has your room all set." Bill stood up and nudged Pete, who was falling asleep. "Ok, baby brother. That was fun. We will see you in the morning. It was more strange than fun, but Devin didn't respond. He wanted to make sure they made their way into the guest bedroom, which was right off the living room. Devin grabbed an extra lantern from the living room and handed it to Bill. Bill called for Bella, who was sound asleep on the kitchen floor. She scurried in as Bill guided her into the guest room. Pete somehow managed to stand as they both headed into the bedroom. The unique thing about the guest room hallway is that in addition to a bedroom door, the hallway had a pocket door, which added an extra level of privacy and prevented noise intrusion from the rest of the house.

Devin watched them stumble into the bedroom and closed the pocket door to the hallway. "Goodnight, you two," he said under his breath, relieved that the strange night was over.

He headed to their bedroom, where he saw Garrett, all settled in and lying right in the middle of the bed. Emily had gotten into her pajamas and said, "I'm going to attempt to clean up the kitchen before we go to bed."

Devin replied and said, "I'll be in to help you. Let me get into my pajamas, and I'll be right out." Emily smiled and headed out the door. Devin looked at Garett as he was deeply involved in a video game. "You tired, bud?" Devin asked. Garrett looked up and said, "Yeah, a little. I keep hearing the storm, though."

"It's ok. We will be right in the kitchen. Put your headphones back on, and you won't hear the wind," Devin tried to say reassuringly.

Devin changed into his pajamas which consisted of sleep shorts and a t-shirt and went in to join Emily in the kitchen. She was rinsing her glasses as Devin surveyed the damage. He looked and saw the entire large bottle of vodka empty. Next to the empty bottle were all the used mixers for the Cosmopolitans that were free flowing all night. The food Emily had put out looked like it was barely touched. So much alcohol was consumed, and there was very little food to absorb it all.

Emily said, "Well, that was a weird night, huh?"

Devin laughed and said, "That is an understatement. I have never seen Jack like that. What was that all about?"

Emily picked up the empty vodka bottle as if to display the culprit.

"No, it was something else," Devin said.

"Something other than alcohol poisoning?" Emily asked.

Devin paused for a moment and said, "I can't put my finger on it, but he was strangely disconnected."

"What does that mean?" Emily inquired.

Devin said, "I'm not sure, but it was like he was another person. I can't explain it. I've seen him drunk before. This was different."

"Your brother and Pete were pretty drunk." Emily said.

Devin answered and said, "Yes, true, but a normal drunk. Jack was acting really weird. More than he usually does. Plus, the whole flirtatious debauchery that was going on was a head trip."

Emily continued to clean up the mess and said, "Well, I'm glad it's over. The storm is so intense. I don't know how much sleep we will get, but it will feel good to curl up in bed."

Devin saw that they cleaned up the best they could under the circumstances. The glow of the small lantern wasn't enough light to give the kitchen a proper cleaning. They decided the rest could wait until morning and began to gather a few more flashlights for the bedroom. As Emily headed back to the bedroom, Devin did one last sweep of the downstairs. He checked the front door and then the sliding glass door in the kitchen. He had to maneuver around the pile of outdoor furniture but managed to check the lock. He knew Emily had squeezed past it earlier when she took Sloan outside. He was glad he checked when he noticed the door was unlocked. He clicked the lock and gave the door a tug. He could hear the wind really howling, and the pool screen enclosure was whistling with the speed of the wind whipping through it. He went back to the bedroom to join Emily, Garrett, and now Dude, who was also in the bed. Emily saw Devin and said, "Do you think Dude and Bella will be okay not going out one last time?"

Devin replied, "They will have to be. There's no way we can take them out now."

Emily acknowledged again, "I can't believe how much everyone drank."

"Yeah, it was a challenge getting my brother and Pete into the bedroom," Devin said with sheer exhaustion.

The glow of fake candles and camping lanterns filled the room as Devin prepared himself for bed. It had been an odd evening, but he was glad it was over. Garett was fighting sleep at this point and finally gave in as he dozed off. Dude was equally as tired and curled up right in the middle of the bed. The storm was really raging outside, and Devin knew they probably wouldn't get much sleep. He also knew he would be battling for real estate on the bed, fighting Garrett and Dude with their kicking legs. Devin leaned over the bed and gave Emily a kiss.

"Goodnight, baby," he said quietly.

"Goodnight, I love you," she replied. Emily knew this was a formality, as sleeping on a normal night wasn't easy for her.

Now, with a hurricane raging outside, it would be impossible. She closed her eyes anyway.

Devin looked at the clock and noticed it was a few minutes past eleven. His head hit the pillow as he closed his eyes, briefly listening to Irma wreak havoc outside. He checked his phone from the nightstand one last time and saw the continuous weather alerts. The storm was going to hang over them most of the night, and a deep sleep was probably not in his future. He had to try to get some rest as he closed his eyes again. Devin realized he was more tired than he thought. He relaxed into a comfortable state.

Before he knew it, his phone was vibrating on the nightstand. He quickly grabbed his phone, thinking it was another weather warning. When he noticed Emily's phone was silent, he looked at his screen. The display showed 'Alan'. Why would his neighbor be calling?

CHAPTER 15

TERROR

Devin shot up in bed as he grabbed his phone and quickly answered it. Emily sat up as well and looked at Devin in confusion. As Devin held the phone to his ear, he said, "Alan? Is everything okay?" Devin could hear commotion in the background as well as Sloan crying. Alan responded and said, "Can you open your door? I need to come back. Something is wrong. Please Devin." The phone went silent, and Devin was in a daze. Emily quickly said, "What's wrong? Is Alan, okay?"

Devin said, "I'm not sure. All he said was to open the door. Something was wrong. Then he hung up, or we got disconnected." Emily looked at Devin and said, "What do you think is wrong?" Devin could no sooner answer her when he heard a loud banging. It was coming from the front of the house, and he quickly realized it was the front door. Emily jumped as Devin raced to the front of the house, grabbing a lantern as he left the room. He quickly peered out of the office window, which was right by the front door, and saw a figure standing there, holding something close to their body. It was dark and hard to make out when it hit him. It was

Alan, holding Sloan. He turned the corner and braced himself to open the door. He knew the wind would be strong and the door could easily fly open. He pushed out as Alan moved out of the way and ran into the house with Sloan. Devin quickly shut the door and looked at Alan. He was soaking wet, and Sloan was wrapped in a blanket. It wasn't the rain-soaked clothes that got Devin's attention, but the blood that was all over both of them. Devin said, "Oh my God. Are you okay? What happened?" Alan, at this point, was sobbing uncontrollably. He was gasping, trying to form words when he finally said, "It's Jack. He went crazy. We were talking about the night, and he snapped. He pushed me, then he started throwing things. When I fell, I hit my head."

Devin could now see, as he held up the lantern closer to Alan, that he was bleeding. He looked at Alan and quickly said, "Is Sloan hurt?" Devin feared that she was injured as he saw the blood-soaked blanket and heard her muffled cries through the cloth. Alan responded, "No, I don't think so. I think the blood is from me."

Emily, after hearing the commotion, ran from the bedroom to the foyer. She saw Alan and Sloan and immediately said, "Oh my God. What is happening? Are you okay?"

Devin quickly said to Emily, "Honey, I will explain in a minute. Can you take Sloan and make sure she is okay?"

Emily didn't hesitate and took the baby from Alan. Right away, she started cradling her as she turned to head to their room to fully inspect her. "Shhhhh, it's ok, little one. Miss Emily has you," she said quietly, heading across the house.

Devin said to Alan, "Start from the beginning. What happened?'

Alan was dazed, in shock, still half drunk, and probably needed some attention to the wound on his head, but Devin needed to access the situation first. Alan said, "He was acting so weird tonight. At first, I thought it was the drinking, but it was something else. I've never seen him like this."

Devin wanted to agree with Alan. Jack was absolutely acting odd, but he didn't want to say anything yet. He wanted Alan to finish his story.

"He kept talking in circles and acting like he was jealous. It came out of nowhere. He has never done anything like this before."

Devin's only thought that something was triggered and escalated as he watched the odd behavior of his brother and Jack. The flirtatious interaction between all of them was apparent all night. Devin said to Alan, "Has he ever hit you or acted violently towards you and Sloan before?"

Alan didn't hesitate and said, "No. Never. It's the weirdest thing. I was so scared when he snapped."

Devin knew Jack could be a little weird, but never in his life did he think he would be standing here discussing an outburst like this.

Alan felt his head and cleared the blood from the gash. As he pulled his hand away, he said to Devin, "I have to go try and talk with him." Devin couldn't believe what he was hearing and responded, "I don't think that is a good idea. I don't know how you walked over here in the storm as it was. Going back isn't a good idea. How did you even leave?"

Alan said, "When he pushed me, I grabbed Sloan, who was on the couch. When we got home, I put her there until we could get settled. Once Jack snapped, he stumbled into the bedroom. I heard him yelling, but I didn't know what he was saying. That's when I called you. Then I bundled Sloan up and ran out of the house."

"So, the last time you saw him, he was in your room?" Devin inquired.

"I think so," Alan said. "Look, I have to try and talk with him. He's my husband, and I don't think he meant to hurt me. When he pushed me, I stumbled, and that's when I hit my head."

Devin wasn't sure what was happening and was still trying to process it all. Alan said, "Can you just hang on to Sloan while I go talk with him?"

Emily walked back into the foyer holding Sloan and said, "She is okay. She's calmer now. She's still a little wet, but she's not hurt. It must have been Alan's blood on her."

Devin said to her, "Jack got a little upset, and they got into some sort of argument. Things got heated, and Jack pushed Alan, and he fell and hit his head."

Emily said to Alan, "Oh, I'm so sorry, Alan. Let me look at your head." Devin was glad the power was still out and they could only see through candle or lantern lights. Emily would have freaked out if she saw the amount of blood on Alan.

Alan said, "No, it's ok. I'm fine. I was just telling Devin I need to go back and talk to Jack."

Emily knew in an instant that she didn't like this idea. The storm was relentless, and it was not safe for him to be going back and forth. Before Emily could protest, Alan said, "Look, I know it sounds crazy, but I need to do this. I'm also worried if he is acting so strangely; what is he capable of doing to himself?"

Emily looked at Devin, and they both couldn't argue that defense. Maybe Jack needed help, and Alan could talk sense into him. Maybe by the time he got back to the house, their quarrel would have blown over, or, with any luck, Jack would have passed out.

Devin said, "Ok, we will keep Sloan here. Go and try to talk some sense into him. If you need me, call me. We miraculously still have cell service."

Alan said, "Ok, I will. He's a good person. I really don't know where this is coming from. I think if I can talk with him, he will calm down."

Devin walked Alan over to the door and braced himself. He knew he would have to fight the wind again. He looked at Alan and said, "Be careful. You can come right back if you need to. Sloan will be fine." Alan nodded and prepared himself for the quick journey back through the storm. Devin opened the door and disappeared into the night and the driving rain.

Emily said, "This is insane. That is not like Jack at all."

Devin said, "Well, I'm sure the five gallons of cosmopolitans they all drank tonight didn't help."

Emily responded and said, "I just hope Alan can talk some sense into him."

Devin didn't want to discuss Jack's emotional state. He knew he was odd, but Emily never really saw it or was oblivious to it. None of it mattered. Here they were standing in their house in the middle of a hurricane, playing couples counselors. Devin thought it would be best for Emily to head back to the room. "Why don't you take Sloan back to our room? I will wait here to see if Alan calls or needs to come back."

Emily was too tired to argue, so she began the walk through the living room, then the kitchen, then to their master bedroom in the back. As she started to walk, Devin asked her, "Did Garrett wake up?"

"No," she replied. "I kept his headphones on with some music before he fell asleep. He's still out cold."

Devin looked at her and signaled to the guest room hallway, "Speaking of out cold, I guess Bill and Pete didn't hear all that commotion. Bella didn't even bark."

Emily shrugged her shoulders, had no response, and continued her way to their bedroom. Devin knew that with the guest room door shut and the hallway pocket door closed, no sound was getting to them. Plus, because of the state they were in, the dead could be woken up easier.

Devin stood in the hallway for a moment and glanced at his phone. His battery was still good, and it still showed two bars of cell service. He would give it a few minutes, and if he didn't hear from Alan, he would join Emily back in the bedroom. He was hoping that Alan was able to talk to Jack, or at the very least make sure he was okay. He no sooner had that thought when he heard a horrific bang against the front door. Devin was standing close enough to it as he jumped what seemed like three feet off the floor. "Jesus Christ," he said out loud. Then another pounding on the door was followed by a yell. He grabbed the handle of the front door and quickly began opening it without thinking. He should have tried to look out of the office window first, but instinct and pure panic kicked in, and he opened the door. The wind grabbed the door and swung it open against the side of the porch wall. Alan came stumbling in out of breath and collapsed on the foyer floor.

As Devin battled the wind to try and get the door shut, a flash of lightning illuminated the side yard. Devin could see a figure standing there. He could make out the shape of a man and knew right away that it was Jack. Devin quickly looked and saw he was holding something in his hand. He didn't want to analyze what it was for too long because he knew he had to get the door closed and locked. As he pulled again, it seemed like the wind was winning when he saw that Jack was now moving towards the porch. Devin pulled as hard as he could this time, the door shutting a little more. As he continued the battle with the door and the wind, the sky flashed again. This time, Jack had made it closer and was now standing on the porch. Devin almost screamed but kept his composure. For a nanosecond, the wind shifted directions as Devin was quickly able to get the upper hand on the door. As he was slamming it shut, he glanced down at Jack's hand and saw the obvious shape of a knife. Once the door was shut, Devin quickly locked it, and as he did, he heard another thud against the door. He knew Jack had reached the threshold and wanted in.

He looked at Alan sobbing on the floor and yelled to him, "What the actual fuck is going on?"

Alan, sniffling, managed to say, "I don't know. I went to talk with him, and he got even angrier. He wasn't making any sense. Then he just screamed, ran to the kitchen, and grabbed a knife. When I saw that, I ran for the door. He almost caught me, but I kicked him. As he was falling, I think he cut himself, but I got out of there as fast as I could."

Devin was still standing against the door, feeling the pounding of Jack's body. The thuds would subside for a few seconds, then could be felt again. Devin knew Jack must have been stepping back a few steps each time and running towards the door. He was trying to knock it in. Devin had cursed having an outward swinging door and vowed to replace it with a door that swung in for years. He was now never happier to have never completed that on his to-do list. The door was thick and tall, and luckily, it had no windows. Kicking a door down that swung in was next to impossible.

Devin continued the conversation with Alan, "So you're telling me your husband has snapped for some odd reason and is now trying to get into my house? Oh, and he also has a knife?"

Alan didn't know what to say because he knew the question was rhetorical. Devin decided to try and deal with this his way and began to try and communicate with Jack through the door. Devin took a deep breath and said, "Look, Jack. I don't know what's going on, but let's talk, ok?"

Devin heard a loud moan from the other side of the door. Jack then started to speak, but Devin could only make out a few words. He heard 'loyalty, milk, wife, baby' There were no other words he could distinguish.

Devin continued, "Jack, it's me. Your neighbor. This isn't you; come on."

More banging started to happen as he could hear Jack yelling. This time it was clearer, and Devin heard, "Give me back my baby!"

Devin yelled, "Jack, look! You need to go home and sleep it off. You're not getting Sloan right now."

Devin heard more noises coming from the door, but this time the banging was replaced by scrapping. Devin wasn't sure what it was at first until he held his ear up against the door. He knew right away that it was the sound of a knife sliding down the outside. Devin's heart was racing so much that he thought it was going to pop right out of his chest.

Devin had to stop Jack somehow so the terror could end.

Jack had stopped throwing himself against the door and was now leaning against it. He wasn't moving and was just scraping the knife against the door. Devin knew he had a chance to catch him off guard. Since his newly beloved door swung outward, Devin could catch him off guard. He couldn't think about it for too long, so he grabbed the handle. He looked at Alan, still on the floor, as if to tell him, 'It's GO time.'

Devin unlocked the door with his other hand and pushed as hard as he could. Jack stumbled backwards but caught himself. Pure adrenaline was rushing through Devin's body as he decided to step out quickly on the porch and shut the door behind him. Devin was now steadying himself so the wind wouldn't blow him over. Devin looked at Jack standing there. The wind sounded like a freight train, and the rain was sideways. He began to yell over the raging storm and said, "Jack! This is my house, and you are not getting in. Do you hear me? Now knock it off and go home."

Devin looked at Jack, who was standing only ten feet from him on the porch. He made eye contact with him as if Devin had gotten through to him. Jack began to turn to walk off the porch and hopefully go home. Just as Devin was about to let his guard down, Jack turned back around and raced toward Devin as he braced for contact. Devin was in his mid-fifties and stayed in pretty good shape, which was about to come in handy. As Jack made it to Devin, he pushed him back with every ounce of strength he had in him. This time it was more force than the door, and it knocked Jack off of the porch and onto the grass in the side yard. The rain was pummeling Jack as he sat there, staring at Devin. Then the yelling began. The non-sequiturs, the cursing, and the yelling for Sloan. Devin felt a slight sting in his arm and thought he must have hurt himself by pushing Jack back so violently. He looked at Jack, who still sat there ranting and screaming. Devin saw a flash from the sky, and this time he saw that Jack didn't have the knife anymore. Another flash, and he saw the knife on the edge of the porch. It obviously dropped out of his hand when Devin pushed him. Devin, in all the fury, completely forgot that Jack had a knife. He looked down at the arm that was stinging and saw it. A three-inch gash in his sleeve with a small blood stain. Jack had cut him as Devin pushed him away. That's when Devin saw Jack move again. He was trying to get up and, most likely, get to the knife. Devin, after feeling overly triumphant and overpowering Jack, knew his middle-aged body couldn't take another exchange. He needed to get back in the house fast. Devin whipped around, opened the door, and locked it quickly behind him as he got back in the house.

He looked at Alan and said, "I understand now; talking it out with him isn't working."

Alan looked like he had crawled through a swamp. He was muddy, bloody, and soaking wet. Devin was shocked at the site. It was only five hours earlier that Alan stood in their kitchen, looking like an ad for a high-end men's clothing store. Now he was broken and confused as he listened to his enraged husband outside. Devin crouched down to Alan and said, "He is not getting into this house, and you are not going anywhere. I want you to sit here in the hallway, and I want you to call 911. Do you hear what I am telling you?" Alan shook his head, yes.

"Do you have your phone?" Devin asked.

Alan wasn't sure as he began to search his body for it.

Devin, running out of patience, said, "Never mind. Here, use my phone." He handed Alan his phone, and as he did, he dialed 911 for him.

"You tell them what's going on, and I will be right back. I'm going to check on Emily and the kids." As Devin turned, he almost fell over Dude, who was now standing there, investigating the commotion. Jack's banging and scrapping against the door seemed to have awoken him. Devin raced to the room as Dude followed along.

When Devin got to the room, Emily was rocking Sloan, and now Garrett was awake.

"What's going on, Dad?" Garrett asked.

Devin answered, "Nothing, son, it's ok."

Emily looked at Devin and knew he couldn't fill her in with Garett's in ear shot. Emily turned to Garrett and said, "Honey, why don't you play a quick game on your iPad? Daddy and I have to check on something."

Garett didn't have to be told twice. It wasn't every day that he got permission to play more games on his iPad, especially so late at night.

Emily stood up with Sloan in her arms and walked into the kitchen with Devin.

Emily said, "Ok, what happened?"

Devin explained, "Alan tried to talk with Jack, but let's just say it didn't go very well."

"What does that mean?" Emily asked.

"Jack is going a little crazy." Devin said. "He chased Alan back over here and is yelling something about Sloan. Alan is back here and is calling 911."

"Oh my God," Emily whispered.

Devin omitted the details about the knife that he saw in Jack's hand. He didn't want to add to her stress. It was dark in the room, so she couldn't see the tear in his sleeve with his blood.

Devin said, "I have to go check on Alan and see if he got through to 911. Take Sloan back into the room and sit with Garrett. Emily went back into the room, and Devin headed back to the foyer. Dude was now at his side again.

When Devin got back to Alan, he saw that he had nodded off with the phone in his lap. Devin grabbed the phone and looked at the screen. It showed 'Dropped Call'.

He stood there for a second and realized that Jack appeared to have stopped his reign of terror. The only noise he was hearing now was the wind and rain. Devin walked into the office and looked out of the window to see the porch. He didn't want to risk shining a flashlight, so he did his best to look. He pressed his face against the window and peered outside. The sky flashed yet again, and Devin could see the porch was empty. Jack wasn't there. Devin wanted to believe he had stumbled home and gone to sleep.

Just then, Devin heard another huge bang. This time, it wasn't coming from the door. It came from inside. He walked out into the foyer from the office and saw Alan now completely passed out on the floor. The small foyer table that Emily found at a local thrift store that sat against the small wall had fallen over. Alan must have hit it as he passed out, and it came crashing down. Devin couldn't deal with

Alan and dialed 911 himself. He was hoping that the call wouldn't drop out. He looked at his phone, and he still had service.

The phone was ringing, and in what seemed like an eternity, an operator picked up. "911 What's your emergency?"

Devin paused for a moment. What was he about to tell them? My gay neighbor is trying to break into my house to get his child. His husband is here, passed out on my floor. Too many cosmopolitans were flowing, and things got out of hand. He stuttered a bit and finally said, "Someone is trying to break into our house." The 911 operator responded, "Do you know this person? Is anyone hurt?"

Devin thought it was odd that she asked if he knew the person but told her, "Well yes, it's our neighbor. He was over earlier with his husband. After they left, he seemed to have snapped. His husband is back here, and so is their child. I'm not sure if my neighbor is okay. I have a small cut on my arm." Devin listened to himself, and it all sounded so crazy. The 911 operator said, "Sir, is everyone safe in the house? Is this person still attempting to break in?"

Devin listened for a moment and realized it had been quiet. He hadn't heard the scraping of the knife against the door or Jack's body slamming against it in a while. Devin focused back on the conversation.

"No, I don't believe so. His husband said he pushed him, and he hit his head. I tried to reason with him, but he charged at me, and I pushed him back. He had a knife."

The 911 operator did what she was trained to do. She asked questions as she typed furiously, getting every detail.

Devin needed some reassurance from her and said, "Ma'am, can you just send someone out? I'm not sure where he is now. Maybe he went back home, but I would feel better if you sent an officer out."

The pause on the other end of the phone spoke volumes. Then she said, "Sir, I'm so sorry. No officers are on the road right now. The storm is just too strong to send anyone. If the storm subsides or weakens, we can send someone, but right now we just can't. It's not safe."

Devin felt sick. He listened to the howling winds and rain again. How could this be? He thought the police were there no matter what to protect and serve. Irma was prohibiting both. He pleaded with her. "Ma'am, please, can anyone come out just to drive by?"

The operator on the other end of the line could hear Devin's desperation, but it was completely out of her control. She said, "Sir, all I can tell you is to be safe, and if the weather changes, we can send someone out."

Devin didn't want to hang up the phone. He felt a little safer knowing she was on the other line, but he knew he had to end the call.

Devin finally responded defeatedly, "Ok, goodbye." When he hit end call on the phone, he felt even more nauseous. He was on his own. He couldn't believe this was happening.

CHAPTER 16

FEAR

Devin knew he had to get back to Emily and Garrett. He was numb at this point but had to focus. He looked at Alan, who was passed out on the foyer floor, then walked through the living room. All of their house guests have now passed out and are sleeping through not only a hurricane but a crazed neighbor trying to get in. He walked into the bedroom and saw Emily on the bed with Sloan and Garrett still playing games on his iPad. Devin saw Garrett had headphones in and could talk to Emily without him hearing.

"What's going on? Are the police coming?" Emily asked hopefully.

"No," Devin said bluntly. "Apparently the storm is so bad they can't send anyone out."

Emily looked at him in disbelief. "What the hell? Are you serious?"

Devin, still in shock, said, "I guess it's standard safety protocol."

Emily then said, "Well, that's just great. What are we supposed to do?"

Devin tried to reassure her. "Look, I think Jack went home. He's not banging on the door anymore. I'm going to sit out in the kitchen on the couch, just in case, and stand guard. The police said if the weather clears, they will come out."

Emily seemed to be comforted a little and then said, "Honey, Sloan needs a diaper change. Did Alan bring the diaper bag back?"

Devin said, "No, all he could manage to do was get himself back here. Oh, by the way, he's passed out in the foyer."

"Of course, he is," Emily said frustratedly. "Ok, I guess I will have to improvise. Sit here with Sloan for a second." She headed into the bathroom with a flashlight as Devin sat on the edge of the bed. He looked at Garrett, then at Sloan. It was one thing to protect his family, but now he was protecting his neighbor's baby from his neighbor. He was so tired that he could barely wrap his head around it all. Emily emerged from the bathroom holding a box of feminine pads. She walked past the bed, went into the closet, and emerged with a small bag. Emily had recently gone through some of Garrett's old clothes and had a few pairs of his underwear that didn't fit him anymore. She shined the flashlight into the bag and grabbed a pair. Devin watched her as her motherly instincts kicked in. She took a pad and some underwear, constructed a makeshift diaper, and began to change Sloan on the bed.

Devin was in awe of her and watched her work her magic. When she was finished, he said to her, "Well, that was impressive."

Emily chuckled and settled Sloan in the middle of the bed as she was falling asleep, exhausted from the events of the evening.

Devin tapped Garrett on the shoulder. Garrett looked up and took off his headphones.

Devin said, "It's getting late, buddy. Why don't you go back to sleep? Mom is going to be here with you and Sloan. Emily explained to Garrett earlier that Sloan was spending the night because they needed to babysit.

Garrett didn't question the simple explanation and accepted it. He liked having Sloan over and settled in as his eyes began getting heavy.

Devin said to Emily, "I'll be right on the couch if you need me." Emily was happy that their room was right off the kitchen, and she knew Devin would be close. She looked at him and smiled slightly. He looked at her with the glow of the lantern on her face. She was so beautiful, and Devin was lucky to be married to her. She was the voice of calm in chaotic moments, and Devin needed that.

Emily got settled into bed. Garrett was in Devin's spot, and Sloan was in the middle. He leaned over, kissed Emily, and said, "Rest if you can. I'm going to shut the door, but I will check on you later. I don't know how much sleep I'm going to be able to get."

Emily said, "Grab one of your pillows before you go and get a blanket from the laundry room."

"I will," Devin replied. He grabbed a pillow, blew her another kiss, and shut the door behind him. He saw that Dude was by his side again. Usually, Dude claimed his spot on the bed with them each night. Devin looked at him and said, "Sorry boy, full house in the bedroom. You and I are out here."

Dude didn't care as long as he was with Devin. He would follow him around the house all the time and eventually settle down near him.

Devin grabbed a blanket from the laundry room and placed it on the couch with his pillow. He decided to take one last walk through the house, just to be sure. He walked to the front door and had to practically step over Alan, who had shifted positions on the floor since the last time he left him. As upset as Devin was, he looked at Alan asleep on the floor and thought he needed to cover him. He walked back into the laundry room and grabbed another blanket. He turned his back to Alan and placed the blanket on top of him.

He made sure the door was locked and took one last look through the office window at the front porch. The wind was still howling, and the rain was coming down hard. It was dark and hard to see, but Devin couldn't see anyone, specifically Jack, standing there.

He went back through the living room and passed by the guest bedroom hallway. Still no stirring from his brother Pete or Bella. He arrived back in the kitchen and checked the sliding glass door one more time, making sure it was locked and secure.

He sat down on the edge of the couch and took his shoes off. He saw Dude look at him, circle a few times, and finally settled on the floor.

Devin laid back and sighed. What an incredibly insane night it was. He just wanted it to be over. He stretched out on the couch and looked at the time. It was almost 1 a.m.

He pulled the blanket over him as his head settled into the pillow. The couch in the little nook where Emily placed it had a nice view out to the pool deck. The shades were shut but cracked just a bit as Devin looked out into the darkness. He heard the wind whistling through the pool screen and the rain pelting the windows. He thought he should at least rest his eyes for a bit. He looked at Dude on the floor next to him. He was fast asleep. Devin closed his eyes and played the evening back in his head. Still in disbelief, he finally settled into a relaxed state. He took some more deep breaths, and after a few minutes, he was as calm as he was going to get.

His relaxation was short-lived as he heard Dude emit a low, muffled growl. Devin knew that Dude would dream occasionally, and he would have to pet him and reassure him. Sometimes Dude would dream that he was running and would kick Emily and Devin in bed. Dude continued to growl softly but remained curled up and seemingly asleep. Devin thought he would tap him slightly to release him from whatever he was dreaming about. Devin sat up so he could reach Dude. As he did, he glanced out the window to the pool patio. Another flash of lightning lit up the house for a moment, and as soon as it did, Devin's heart almost stopped. There, at the sliding glass door, was a figure. Dude wasn't dreaming, but his canine senses were alerted as he sensed something was wrong.

Fear washed over Devin as he slumped back down on the couch. He peered slowly through the blinds and saw Jack standing there. His back was to him as he stood there, close to the sliding glass door. Then Devin heard the most frightening sound he would ever want to hear. The door latch was moving back and forth. Jack was trying to get in through the back.

CHAPTER 17

SURVIVAL

The notion that Jack had gone back to his house and passed out was gone. Devin lay there frozen as he heard the door latch being manipulated. He wasn't sure what Jack's end game was at this point, and Devin was afraid to find out.

Jack had obviously given up on breaching the front door and was now focused on the back. Devin had thought he had locked the two screen doors that led into the pool area from the side yard. Nevertheless, Jack was in the back area and obviously trying to get into the house. Devin looked at the bedroom door and was hoping that Emily or even Garrett didn't wander out. Devin slinked down even lower on the couch, hoping that Jack wouldn't shift his focus to the window. Devin didn't want him to know that he was there. Devin made his way to the floor, then stood up slowly against the wall right by the patio door. He carefully peered out and saw Jack looking down at the handle. It was so dark that Devin could barely see what he was doing. All he heard was the rattling of the handle. Devin had to think fast. He needed something to protect himself. He didn't own a gun, but he never wished he had one more at this moment. He wasn't against guns or people who owned them; he just never felt the need for one. Tom had always told his dad that if he ever needed one, he could help him. Tom was a gun enthusiast and knew the safe and proper way to handle firearms. He should have listened to his son. He needed a weapon now more than ever in his life.

Devin's heart was racing, and he knew if Jack somehow got in, it would not end well for anyone. He looked around for something to protect himself. All he could think of was to run to the garage and grab a golf club out of his bag. His clubs were just on the other side of the door that led into the garage from the house. He needed to act fast and darted towards the garage door. He quickly opened the door and rummaged through his clubs. Which club should he use? It was almost comical in a moment of panic. He wasn't on the back nine trying to determine which club would get the ball to the green. He needed to just grab a club. Devin grabbed his seven iron and raced back through the house to his original position. He hugged the wall again and tried not to move the blinds that were closed against the sliding glass door.

He listened as Jack was, what seemed like, surgically trying to remove the handle. Devin saw the small path that he had kept open to access the door. All the area around the door had pool furniture, a couple of planters, a chest that kept some pool supplies in it, and some pool noodles. Devin stood there frozen, as Jack was relentless. Just as Jack tried to beat the front door down, he was equally determined on this door. This door was more vulnerable and mostly glass. Devin was afraid that Jack would find something and simply break the glass. He could only think that, in the dark, there was nothing he could find, plus all the items that he could have used were now inside the house.

Devin thought if Jack had a knife, he still would need a lot of force to shatter the glass. Devin heard more rattling and then what sounded like a piece of metal falling.

Devin, for a moment, thought he could whip open the door and overtake Jack. He stopped that thought when he ran the outcome through his head. If Devin committed to that, there was no turning back, and he could end up killing Jack.

Or if he couldn't overtake him, Jack had a knife. He could stab Devin, leaving him incapacitated and the door open for him to get in the house. There was no good choice. Devin thought about the knife that Jack had and looked in the kitchen. He thought what an idiot he was. Devin could have saved the trip to the garage and just grabbed a knife from the kitchen to protect himself. Instead, he stood there with a seven-iron, waiting for the door to slide open, where he would have to face off with Jack. He again ran through the scenario and thought to himself, Maybe the golf club was a better choice. If he had to defend himself, a knife would be more horrific. He was once again in complete disbelief that he was in this situation. He was debating in his mind the best way he might have to kill or hurt his neighbor. A neighbor who just the other day brought them cookies. Now Devin stood there with his heart pounding and sweat dripping down his forehead, followed by shallow breaths. He was in the middle of a horror movie, but this was real life. Devin knew Jack was only seconds away from somehow getting the handle off the door. For someone who was so inebriated, it was baffling to Devin how he was methodically trying to get in.

Devin inched closer to the door and looked down at the handle. The inside lever was still attached, but as he looked closer, he could see the bottom lock was now gone, and he could see through it. A quarter-sized opening scared the hell out of Devin. He knew Jack could still not get in unless he could somehow break the deadbolt. The door had a fail-safe lock above the bottom one. As long as Jack couldn't break the glass, Devin was still safe for the time being.

Devin raised the golf club as he heard more rattling. If Jack did get in, it would be all over. Jack's life could come to an end, and so would Devin's. Killing a man, even in self-defense, would be a traumatizing event, but Jack was not getting into Devin's house. His family's safety was at stake, and he would do everything in his power to protect them.

Devin looked at himself for a moment and saw the seven-iron displayed in the air. At that same moment, he looked at the hole where Jack had removed the bottom lock. It was just big enough for Devin to fit the golf club handle in. If Devin could get close enough, he could slowly slide the handle into the opening and, at the right moment, jab the handle into Jack's torso. Devin knew the soft-handled grip on the club wasn't enough to deter Jack. Devin slipped down low again, slithered into the kitchen, and grabbed a knife from the block on the counter that housed all the other cutlery. He sat down on the floor with his seven iron and quickly cut off the grip, rendering it an open-ended, jagged pole. He slithered back to the door again, careful not to disturb any of the items stacked near it. He didn't want Jack to know he was on the other side of the door.

This was insanity. How could Jack be so violently determined to get in? It didn't matter at that point because the truth was that Jack wanted in, and Devin had to stop him.

Devin stayed low and peered out again through the small opening in the sliding door blinds. This time, he could see Jack's body fully up against the door, still working on the handle. Devin needed to act quickly. He took his once prized seven iron and aligned it with the hole that formerly housed the lock. He knew he had one shot to catch Jack off guard. If he missed or Jack heard him, who knows what his next move might be? Devin was now as low as he could possibly be with the seven iron in place. Devin waited to hear the jiggle again. He knew that once he heard it, Jack was guaranteed to be leaning directly against the door.

Devin heard the wind howling again as Irma was in top form. He listened carefully to the noises of the storm when he heard the handle rattle again. Just as he did with all his might, he jabbed the jagged makeshift lynx dagger through the hole. As he did, he knew immediately that it had hit its target. Devin heard the scream, which turned into a moan, then silence. Devin's quest for his survival and the survival of his family had now been elevated to another level.

CHAPTER 18

RELENTLESS

Devin waited a moment and tried to listen carefully to see if he heard Jack again. The rain and wind were so loud, he had to really concentrate. Devin looked down at the golf club that he pushed into Jack and saw that there was some blood on the end. It wasn't enough to think that Devin caused a huge injury to Jack, but maybe enough to deter him. Devin needed to peek out the window again to check on Jack's position. Every time Devin moved throughout the house, he kept any flashlight or lantern off. He didn't want Jack to know where he was. The only light he had to rely on was his cell phone light, which he kept low as he changed locations.

He needed to make his way closer to the window by the sliding glass patio door. That was a good vantage point and allowed Devin to see if Jack was still by the door. He got down low and made his way closer to the window. Devin was hoping a flash from the sky would illuminate the corner of the pool deck enough. Lighting hardly ever occurred during a hurricane but was proving to be a welcome addition, allowing Devin to catch quick glimpses of the outside. He was finally putting Emily's father's weather facts to use. He remembered him talking about lighting during a hurricane, which, although rare, was a sign of rapid intensification. It certainly appeared that this was coinciding with Irma, as the storm was becoming louder and angrier.

Devin was baffled at how Jack was functioning and maneuvering in the heavy wind and rain. Was it the alcohol? Was he high on something else? Devin moved to the window and slowly cracked open the blinds, waiting for another flash. He didn't have to wait long when the sky quickly lit up. Jack was gone and not standing by the door any longer. Hopefully, he abandoned the task of dismantling the door handle from outside. Devin was still confused about how he was doing it. The handle from the outside had two rivets that you couldn't pull off, but Jack managed to do it somehow. Devin hoped the jab to Jack's torso sent a message and forced him home. Devin wanted another vantage point to look outside. He knew if he went upstairs and peered out Garrett's window and if he lucked out with another lighting flash, he could get a good view of the side yard. Before he could do that, he needed to find something to seal up the hole where the bottom door lock once lived.

He looked at the sea of items he had placed in the dining room and saw some duct tape he had. So many people in Florida thought if they duct taped their windows, it would prevent the windows from breaking during a storm. This proved to be false because if a broken tree branch was picked up by the intense hurricane winds, it would crash through with ease. Devin used his duct tape for other projects around the house. He recently used it for the pool vacuum hose, which had a small tear in it. He had left it outside, and when he pulled in the pool furniture, he grabbed it and put it on the kitchen table. He took the tape, tore off a piece, and placed it over the hole. He kept tearing pieces apart and adding layers to cover the hole even more. He wasn't sure what good it was doing other than keeping any rain that could blow in through the small hole. Devin looked at the pile of pool furniture and decided to push as much as he could directly against the door to add another layer of protection in case Jack was devising a plan to crash through. Devin got down on the floor, placed his feet on the back of the table, and pushed. Now the table with all the pool furniture and outside objects was directly against the door.

Devin shot up and used the glow of his phone to make his way across the house to the stairs. He ran up the stairs and immediately went into Garrett's room to look out the window. This time, when he waited, he wasn't fortunate enough to get a flash of light to illuminate the yard. He peered out and still couldn't see anything. He knew he had to get back downstairs. Devin raced back down the stairs and made his way to the foyer. Once again, he stepped over Alan, who was still passed out on the floor. He went into the office and quickly looked out into the darkness, trying to see if he could see Jack. Still nothing. He made his way back around the corner and headed back to the kitchen. As he made his way into the room, his bedroom door opened. His heart started to race even more when he saw Emily standing there, as if she saw a ghost. She looked at Devin and quietly whispered, "He's trying to get into our bedroom window."

Devin felt the heat rush through his body, and a complete panic set in. He looked at the open bedroom door and saw the glow of a lantern that Emily had on. He quickly snapped at Emily in an aggressive, hushed tone and said, "Turn off the lamp!"

Emily quickly went back in, with Devin following closely behind. He could see that Garrett was still in bed with Sloan. Emily went to her nightstand and turned off the lamp. As she did, Garrett, now awake again, whimpered, fighting back tears, and said, "Dad, he's at the window."

Two windows flanked the king-sized bed. The window on the left, where Garrett lay, is where the sound was coming from. Devin turned to Emily and whispered, "Take the kids and get in the closet and lock it behind you." Emily didn't hesitate, grabbed the baby, and told Garrett to follow her. Devin grabbed the pillows and a blanket, threw them in the closet, and shut the door behind them. He made his way over to the window and tried to listen to see if Jack was trying to break the window lock. It was inconceivable to Devin that Jack was still at it and determined to get into the house. Just as the storm was relentless, Jack was equally so trying to break in. He got closer to the window and heard an odd sound. It was almost as if fingernails were being scraped down the screen, but as Devin listened closer, he knew it wasn't fingernails. Jack was using a knife and slicing through the screen.

CHAPTER 19

ADRENALINE

Devin looked down at his phone and thought he could try 911 again. The storm had only gotten stronger, and the decision not to send emergency services out was probably still standing. He felt completely alone and needed help. His family was locked in a closet, his house guests were incapacitated, and there was Dude who was shaking more than the trees in the wind outside. He dialed 911 again, but this time nothing happened. He looked closer at the dim glow of the phone display and saw it had no signal. He suddenly remembered that the house line could be his only hope. He grabbed the phone from the cradle and turned it on. Not surprisingly, the phone was dead. A mixture of anger, fear, and sheer exhaustion ran through his body. He noticed the sound of the blade running down the screen had stopped. Devin wasn't assuming anymore that Jack was stopping. No sooner did he think that when he heard the same sound of the screen being cut on the opposite window. This time, a new sound was added as Devin heard the tapping of the knife blade on the window. It was a distinct sound, and Devin knew Jack was still at it. It was such an incredibly eerie sound, and once again, Devin felt like he was in the middle of a nightmare.

Devin needed to make a decision. Jack had to be stopped. He thought for a moment that he needed to find his way outside and confront Jack. He would have to brave the elements, overtake him, and put an end to this madness. How could this even be happening? He was contemplating overtaking his neighbor in the middle of a hurricane. Then what? Again, he was faced with an unfathomable decision. Kill or be killed? Was this even in Devin's DNA?

He needed to devise a plan. He would have to go out the front door, fight the incredible storm, find Jack, and determine a way to take him down. When he ran the scenario through his head, it sounded absurd. Something had to be done. For whatever reason, Jack was not giving up. He wanted in, either to harm everyone in the house, harm Alan, grab Sloan, or perhaps all the above.

Devin tapped slightly on the closet door and whispered to Emily.

"I am going outside to find him. He is not stopping, and I need to make sure we put an end to this." Emily quickly whispered back, "Devin, do not go outside. You can't. The storm is so strong right now, and who knows what Jack could do?"

Devin knew Emily was probably right, but what other choice did he have? He heard Garrett crying softly through the door. Sloan managed to stay asleep through the craziness of being shuffled into the closet. Devin knew Emily was talking to Garrett and comforting him, but still, his muffled cries cut through Devin. He was getting angry that this was upsetting and scaring his family. The adrenaline raced through his body as he leaned against the door and said to Emily, "Do not open this door no matter what. Do you understand? Stay in there until I come back."

Emily was trying to stay calm and adamantly said, "Devin I am begging you, do not leave the house." Emily did not get a reply because Devin was already on his way to the front door.

By now, the house was shaking as Irma was showing her true strength. Devin approached the door and walked through the plan in his head. If he was heading outside, he would take a flashlight. This time, he didn't care if Jack saw him. That was the point. Begin the showdown and let it play out. Take him down, no matter what. Stop his once friendly, pleasant, and subdued neighbor now turned insane maniac. Devin grabbed the door handle and heard the wind howling stronger than it had been all night. The gusts predicted by the meteorologists to be up to one hundred and twenty-five miles per hour were now coming to fruition.

Devin took a flashlight from the hallway table next to the door, took a deep breath, grabbed the door handle, and readied himself for what he could face outside.

CHAPTER 20

DAWN

Emily sat in the closet with the kids, waiting for Devin to return. Ten minutes had passed, which seemed like ten hours. She listened to the wind beating against the house. Even though the closet had no windows, she could hear the house breathing and fighting the elements. Garrett had calmed down and was resting his eyes, leaning against Emily for comfort. Sloan was still soundly asleep on the blanket Emily had laid out. Emily had brought the lantern in with her and knew it was safe to turn it on. She sat in the warm glow and contemplated the irony of the safe setting compared to the mayhem outside. She wanted everything to be over. The thought of Devin outside was not only terrifying but also overwhelming. What state was Jack still in, and what was he capable of?

As Emily ran every horrible scenario through her head, she heard something on the other side of the door. A crashing sound came from her side of the bed, near the window. Emily wanted to scream but knew she couldn't risk scaring Garrett or waking Sloan. She sat there, frozen, listening for any other noise. She felt sick at the thought of Devin outside looking for Jack, but now he could be inside the house. As scared as she was, anger made its way in at Devin for trying to be a hero. Jack could be in their bedroom right now, and Devin could be hurt outside, leaving her completely vulnerable.

She sat as still as she possibly could when she heard a tap on the door. She gasped as she heard a voice on the other side. This can't be happening, she thought, and she tried not to make any audible sound. She anticipated the door would come crashing in, and she would have to think fast. As she braced herself, she heard Devin whisper on the other side of the door. "Emily. Emily, it's me."

Emily was never happier to hear Devin's voice.

"Oh my God, Devin. What the hell happened?"

Devin placed his face closer to the door. "I never went outside. I thought about it, and I got close, but the storm is so strong right now that I couldn't risk it. If I went out and he overtook me and got in, I could never forgive myself."

Emily responded, "I heard a crash in the bedroom. What was that?"

Devin wasn't sure what she was referring to and held his phone up to look around. As he surveyed the room, he saw on the floor Emily's water glass, which must have been too close to the edge and had fallen off.

"It was your water glass," Devin reassured her.

Emily thought earlier that when she first heard Jack trying to get into the window, she hastily placed her glass on the nightstand. She didn't realize how close to the edge it probably was. A huge wave of relief came over her. Devin was safe in the house, and Jack was hopefully still outside, or maybe with any luck at home by now.

Devin said to Emily, "Why don't you crack open the door and let some more air in? It must be stuffy in there."

Emily hadn't really thought about it, but she realized it was true when he said it. The sweat of a ten-year-old boy and the saturated makeshift diaper on Sloan were overtaking the small space. Emily opened the door and saw Devin. He reached in and touched her face for reassurance and said, "I am going to look around and check all the windows again. I haven't heard anything in a while."

Emily nodded as Devin went off to check the house. He passed through the kitchen and looked at the time on his phone. It was already four a.m. There are just a couple more hours until dawn, and hopefully the storm will be weakening by then. Devin checked every window and tried to peer outside. He still couldn't see anything but noticed the wind was not as strong, and the rain seemed to be weakening but still steady.

Devin made his way back to the bedroom and reported his findings to Emily.

"It seems like the storm is possibly weakening. I am not hearing anything else from around the house, but I am going to stay right here. If you're okay, let's keep you guys in the closet until we know for sure Jack has given up."

Emily agreed with Devin and decided to keep the door cracked. Devin grabbed a pillow and sat down next to the closet door. Before he could get settled, he got up again. "I'll be right back," he said to Emily, and he made his way to the kitchen. Devin returned in no time, but this time he had a knife in his hand. He sat back down and placed it next to him.

Emily whispered to Devin, "Is Alan still asleep in the foyer? Did your brother or Pete wake up at all?"

Devin simply said, "Nope. Everyone is sleeping through the chaos."

Emily shook her head in disbelief, then Devin said,

"I'm just going to sit here. The best thing we can do is wait until dawn. Maybe the phone lines will be back, and we can call the police again."

Emily knew they wouldn't be able to sleep but felt better knowing Devin was by their side. Dude, who was in his bed on the other side of the room, got up and curled up next to Devin. Emily reached through the small door opening and took Devin's hand as they sat there, waiting for dawn to come.

CHAPTER 21

AFTERMATH

Devin's head jerked awake as he found himself coming out of sleep. He pushed the closet door open a bit and saw Emily, Garrett, and Sloan sound asleep. He stood up and went to the window, where he saw the first light of day breaking the horizon. Through the window, he saw the tattered screen that Jack had slashed. The storm had passed, and Devin could tell that it was raining slightly and a little breezy. Nothing compared to Irma's rage hours earlier.

Devin made his way out of the room and to the front of the house as Dude followed him. As he approached the foyer, he saw that Alan was gone and no longer asleep on the floor. Devin saw the front door was unlocked and quickly secured the deadbolt. Alan must have woken up and left. Devin was angry that he just walked out and left the door unlocked but realized he was probably still drunk. Devin went back into the bedroom as Emily was emerging from the closet.

"Sorry, I didn't mean to wake you", Devin said.

Emily quickly answered, "Trust me, there was no sleep involved in the last two hours. I was just resting. I heard you get up. You dozed off for about twenty minutes. Where did you just go?"

Devin said, "I went to check the house out and saw that Alan was gone. The front door was unlocked."

Emily said, "Oh my god, for how long do you think?"

"Probably not long" Devin said. "When I checked around four, he was still there. It's five forty-five now, so he must have left not long ago."

"Any sign of Jack?" Emily cautiously asked.

"Not that I saw," Devin answered.

Devin didn't share his fears with Emily. His worst fear is that he will go outside and see Jack's lifeless body floating in the pool. Jack was so incredibly out of his mind that anything was possible. Did he fall, hit his head, and stumble into the pool in the darkness? Did he fall on his knife and bleed to death? Any one of those scenarios could have been possible given the events that unfolded last night.

Devin said to Emily, "It will be fully light soon. I'll go out and inspect the house."

The power was still out, but as the sun was slowly coming up, the lanterns were no longer needed. The house felt stuffy after being without air conditioning for almost ten hours, but Devin was happy to see the morning light approach.

Emily said to Devin, "Sloan is going to wake up soon. She will be hungry and desperately in need of a diaper change. A real one, not the ones I created."

Devin agreed and then said, "I'm not sure where Alan went, but he has to be coming back for Sloan."

Emily was afraid to ask but spoke anyway: "Devin, what if Alan went home to check on Jack and he hurt him?"

Devin had to admit the thought had crossed his mind, but he couldn't deal with it. He said to Emily, "I am sure he is fine." As Devin was about to produce some more comforting words, he heard a bang coming from the front door. They both jumped a bit and looked at each other. Devin said, "Wait here." He ran to the front office and looked out the window. Daylight was now making it easier to see. As he looked out, he saw Alan standing there, holding a diaper bag. Devin made his way to the door and opened it.

"Are you ok, Alan?" Devin asked.

"Yes, yes, I'm ok. Is Sloan, okay?" Alan responded.

"She is fine. She is with Emily but will be getting up soon and will need to be fed. Alan, where is Jack?" Devin asked.

Alan said, "I don't know. I woke up this morning and went home to check. He is not there."

Devin's fear of finding Jack's body somewhere in his yard was now coming to the forefront of his mind again.

"Where the hell do you think he is?" Devin snapped.

"I don't know," Alan said sheepishly.

Devin now felt the need to unleash on Alan and said, "Look, Alan, your husband terrorized us last night. I don't know what the hell is going on with him or what happened, but you need to find him. I need to know my family is safe. You were passed out most of the night as we were dealing with your husband who turned into Jack Nicholson from The Shining last night.

Alan looked at Devin and said, "I know Devin. I am so sorry this happened. If you can hang on to Sloan for a bit longer, I would appreciate it. I have diapers and a bottle here in the diaper bag. I just need to make some phone calls to see if I can track Jack down."

Devin couldn't believe what he was hearing but knew it was probably the safest thing to do, not knowing where Jack was.

Alan said, "Look, I will be back as soon as I can to get Sloan." Then he turned and headed over to his house.

Devin shut the door and went back to Emily, holding the diaper bag. "That was Alan. He brought this for Sloan. He asked if we could watch her for a bit longer until he could track down Jack. We still don't know where he is."

Emily said, "Oh my god. I hope he is okay."

Devin couldn't believe that Emily was feeling compassion for Jack after all that he put them through, but that was Emily. She was a nurturer through and through, so her response didn't surprise him too much.

Garrett started to stir and then sat up and asked, "Is Irma over?" Emily hugged him and said, "Yes, baby. The worst part is over. We still don't have power, but why don't you rest in bed and play on your iPad until we can figure out breakfast for you?" Emily felt a wave of guilt run through her. For the entire night, she used the iPad to distract Garett, but she knew it was the only way to shield him from what was happening.

Emily knew it was still too early for Garrett to think about breakfast, but it was something to say to comfort him. Garrett hopped into bed as Emily grabbed some diapers from the bag for Sloan and started the overdue changing process.

Devin said, "Now that it's light out, I'm going to check the yard for debris." Devin said debris to Emily, but he really was thinking he was going out to check the yard for Jack's body.

 Devin made his way to the sliding glass door and pushed the table away that he had pushed up as a barrier earlier. He opened the blinds to let some light in and reached for the handle.

He managed to jiggle the lock above the smaller one that Jack dismantled in his attempt to get in. As Devin tried to turn the lock, the entire handle and remaining lock fell to the ground. He managed to slide the door open, and as he did, he noticed the door handle and other pieces all strewn on the patio. As he focused on the broken lock, he almost missed the handprints and blood streaks that painted the door glass. Obviously, Jack's blood came from either Devin's jab of the golf club into him, or a knife cut he obtained in his fury. No sooner did that thought run through Devin's mind when he saw on the ground a knife next to the pieces of the door lock and handle. The knife had blood on it and looked like Jack had used it to pry the outer part of the sliding glass door lock. Devin couldn't believe how dangerously close Jack was to getting in through the door. If Jack had jiggled the handle just a bit more, he would have been in the house. Perhaps Devin's seven irons into Jack's body stopped him from continuing and forced him to move to the windows.

As Devin turned the corner, he feared looking into the pool. He thought for sure he would see Jack floating, but as he looked, he thankfully didn't see him. He did, however, look at the wall between the pool door and the other windows. More of Jack's blood was smeared all over. Devin couldn't tell if Jack was intentionally trying to paint with his wound or just used the wall to hold himself up in his demonic state. As Devin looked at all the blood, he looked at the window screens. All of them at the back of the house by the pool were slashed. As Devin continued the inspection of the pool area, he made his way to one of the pool screen doors. The screened door leading into the pool was completely cut open. Devin reached up and realized the pool door was never locked, but Jack never even attempted to try the handle. In his rage, he just cut through the door. The opening through the door wasn't enough for his insatiable rage, so Jack randomly slashed other panels of the pool enclosure to gain access.

Devin looked out into the side yard closest to their bedroom, where Jack had attempted to get in. He looked in the side yard and couldn't believe his eyes. There he saw about a half-dozen knives stabbed into the ground, all with blood on the handles and some on the blades. He continued to inspect the yard and saw that some of the vinyl fence panels that separated their yard and Alan and Jack's yard were strewn about the yard. Devin wasn't certain if the wind from Irma had caused them to blow in or if Jack had pushed through them. Devin thought it must have been a combination of both because he saw more bloody hand prints on some of the panels. Devin looked over at the pool heater and noticed that all the wires were ripped from the wall. The fuse panel was also damaged and dangling by a single wire. Devin could only think that Jack thought it was the power supply to the house and was attempting to cut the power, even though it had been off for hours before Jack went on his rampage. He saw another access panel that housed the phone and internet lines dangling from the wall. That, too, had blood all over it. Before he could go on, he stopped himself. He didn't want Garrett wandering outside to see this. He headed back inside and went into the bedroom. Emily was feeding Sloan with the bottle Alan had packed in the bag. Garrett was diligently battling space creatures in his latest video game.

Devin said to Emily, "Can I talk to you for a second?"

Emily knew that meant an out-of-ear shot conversation from Garrett. Sloan was just finishing up her bottle as Emily took it from her. She turned to Garrett and said, "Can you watch Sloan for a second? I'm going to talk to Dad in the kitchen." Garrett looked up and said, "Sure," and began to cuddle with Sloan.

Devin walked out into the kitchen with Emily.

"What's wrong?" Emily asked.

Devin quietly said, "It looks like a crime scene outside. Do me a favor and make sure Garrett doesn't come out until I can get some of it cleaned up."

Emily looked horrified and could barely respond but finally said, "Are you kidding me?"

Devin said, "Yeah, Jack went to town on the windows and pool screen and left a knife collection in the yard. It looks like someone was filming a slasher movie in our backyard."

They both stood there, completely numb, when another knock on the door startled them. This time Emily followed Devin as they both peeked out the office window to the porch. There, they saw a police officer standing there. Devin turned to Emily and said, "Well, it's a little late for them." They walked around the corner, pushed the door outward, and greeted the officer.

The officer immediately said, "Good morning. We received a call late last night but couldn't come out because of the storm. We are just doing a follow-up. Is everything okay? The report says attempted break-in."

Devin didn't know where to begin but said, "Yes, sir. We believe our neighbor either had too much to drink or was experiencing a psychotic episode and tried to break in and attack us."

The officer responded, "What do you mean when you say attacked?'

Devin didn't want to relive the story but said, "Our neighbors were here for a little party, and they left and went home. At one point, the husband of our neighbor came back injured and said his husband went crazy. Then our neighbor having the episode tried to get in, but I pushed him back. I saw that he had a knife. The rest of the evening he attempted to break in, and this morning I saw a lot of damage to our house and multiple knives stabbed in the yard." Devin heard it all come out of his mouth and even lived through it, but still couldn't believe it.

The officers looked at him and Emily and said, "Do you know where he is now?"

Emily chimed in and said, "No, but his husband was here because we watched their little girl last night while all of this was unfolding. He left early this morning but came back with some diapers. I believe he is looking for his husband now."

Devin said, "Look, officer, could you go over to their house and check? They live right there," as Devin pointed to Alan and Jack's house.

The officer looked at Devin and Emily and said, "Sir, we can't just ask to go in. Right now, there is nothing to go on, and we aren't allowed to go into the house."

Devin was becoming angry and was so overcome with exhaustion and emotions. He looked at them and said, "Nothing to go on? What about the blood, the cut screens, and the knives?" Devin knew it was probably useless because they had to hear both sides of the story and make statements. For all the officers knew, Devin was the one telling a lie and covering something up. They couldn't just react to a one-sided story.

Devin continued, "Sir, I was the one who made the call last night. Can't you do anything?"

The officer responded and said, "Yes, but until we get all the facts, we have to wait. I mean, it's obvious something happened here. I noticed your door when I walked up." Since the door opened, Devin didn't know what the officer was talking about. He stepped out on the porch and looked at the door. Long cuts were gouged into the door, obviously made by one of the knives Jack had.

"Jesus Christ," Devin said. More of Jack's calling card, he thought to himself. He knew Jack was using the knife last night but had no idea of the damage he caused.

Emily knew she had to get back and check on Sloan, so she dismissed herself. "I will be right back," she said, and she went back to the room.

The officer said, "Have you been fighting with your neighbors?"

Devin looked at him and defiantly said, "No! We are all good friends. Something snapped in him. We are not sure what happened."

"Were there any other witnesses?" The officer asked.

Devin almost forgot that his brother and Pete were still asleep in the guest room. He said, "Well, my brother and husband are here, but they were pretty drunk and slept through everything last night." Devin heard the explanations and answers coming out of his mouth and knew that it all sounded weird to the officer. Just as the officer was taking it in, he got a call on his radio attached to his belt. "Excuse me," he said, and he walked off the porch into the driveway to take the call.

As the officer listened to the call, Emily arrived back in the hallway, holding Sloan. "What's going on?' She asked.

"I don't know," Devin replied. "I tried to explain further, but it all sounds crazy."

Devin and Emily looked out of the open door and saw Alan walking back over from his house. He walked on to the porch and said, "I can take Sloan back. I made some calls to some friends, but no one knows where Jack is, and they haven't seen him." Emily could see Alan was scared but didn't say anything and handed Sloan to him.

"Let me grab her diaper bag," Emily said, running back to the bedroom.

Devin looked at Alan and said, "Your husband left quite a calling card last night. Our house probably looks worse from Jack than it does from Irma. What the hell happened, Alan?"

Alan, fighting back tears, said, "I wish I knew. I have never seen him like this. Look, if there is damage, I will pay for it."

Devin snapped, "You know Alan. I don't even care about that at this point. Jack went fucking crazy and tried to break into our house and could have killed us, or I could have killed him."

Emily arrived back with the diaper bag and handed it to Alan. She said to him, "Are you okay?"

All Alan could do was shake his head slightly up and down. The officer had finished his radio call and walked back to the porch.

Devin said to him, "Sir, this is our neighbor's husband. He was the one who came back to our house last night after Jack went berserk."

Alan looked at him and said, "Officer I don't know where he is. I don't think he went home last night. He was here, then went crazy. Maybe it was the drinking, or maybe something else."

The officer listened, then asked Alan if he could describe Jack and what he was wearing last night. Alan began describing Jack, and before he could say anything else, he stopped him and said, "Sir, I just got a call from a colleague of mine on patrol this morning, about five miles from here. He knew about the initial call that came in last night but was responding to a separate call from the owner of a local farm. Apparently, they found a man fitting your husband's description. He was standing in the field, uh, talking to a cow. When the officer approached him, he was saying something about cookies and milk. He looks pretty beat up, has some cuts on his hands, is soaking wet, has ripped clothes, and is full of mud."

Alan looked at the officer and said, "Where is he now?"

The officer responded and said, "Right now he is in the back of a patrol car. We need to make a positive identification of him, and he will probably need some psychiatric evaluation. I can have my colleague drive over here so you can make sure it's him. If you identify him, we can release him to you." He turned to Devin and said, "Sir, if it is him, and we have every reason to believe it is, you can press charges if everything checks out."

Alan stood slightly behind the officer, holding Sloan. Tears were coming down his face, but Devin didn't care. He was still so angry at what unfolded last night. His family was in jeopardy, and Jack put them through hell. He looked at the officer and wanted to say, "Yes, I want to press charges. Let him sit in a cell for a couple of days. Let him think about what he put me and my family through."

Emily saw the look in Alan's eyes as he seemed too non-verbally plead with Devin not to press charges. Emily, who was standing right next to Devin, gently squeezed his arm as a signal to say don't. Devin looked at the officer and reluctantly said, "No, that won't be necessary, officer."

Alan mouthed the words 'Thank you' to Devin.

The officer said, "Well, if you change your mind, you have every right too. I am going to my car to grab my card if you do change your mind." He looked at Alan and said, "My colleague is on his way with your husband. I would advise that you get him checked out. I have to say that in all my years of being a police officer, I have never seen someone walk in a major hurricane five miles and not be dead right now. He was battling winds over one hundred miles per hour. It was completely baffling to me. He is a lucky man." Then he walked to his patrol car.

Devin thought to himself how right the officer was. Lucky indeed. Jack was so close to being seriously hurt or killed if he succeeded in getting into the house. Then he walks into a hurricane and ends up in a field talking to a cow.

Alan began to speak, but Devin stopped him right away and said, "Look, I don't know what happened with Jack last night, and I'm not sure I want to know. All I know is that I have been ridiculously drunk before and never had the urge to terrorize a family. He needs help, Alan, and I only hope he has never hurt you before or does anything like this again. I am not pressing charges out of respect for you and Sloan, but not for Jack. As far as I'm concerned, he's dead to me. I am done. This was more than a drunken mishap. You will pay for all the damages, but we are done here. You tell him I don't want him looking at me, saying hello to me, or engaging in any type of exchange. We are no longer neighbors but simply people who live next to one another. You tell him this, or I will personally tell him myself. Do you understand what I am saying?"

Alan looked at Devin, then looked at Emily and said, "Yes, I understand, but I love him, and I have to forgive him." Devin paused for a second, then said, "But I don't". Alan looked at him for a moment, then turned around with Sloan in his arms and walked away.

Devin waited for the officer to return with his card. As the officer approached, he handed Devin his information and said, "It's none of my business, but if it were me, I would press charges. He could have really hurt someone."

Devin said, "Thank you, officer. We will take it into consideration."

The officer responded, "I will be out in my car and will wait for my colleague to bring your neighbor back. If you're not pressing charges, you don't have to come out and identify him."

"Thank you again, officer." Devin half-heartedly responded and shut the door.

As Devin and Emily turned to walk back through the house, they heard the pocket door from the hallway that led to the guest room. Bill, Pete, and Bella emerged as Bill said chipperly, "Good morning! How did everyone sleep?"

CHAPTER 22

EXHAUSTION

Emily and Devin were too tired to explain to Bill and Pete the events of the evening. The power was still out, the house was hot, and they were completely overwhelmed with the clean-up that awaited them. Bill said to Pete, "Bella must be bursting. I have to let her out." Bill escorted Bella to the back door to let her out, and Pete followed.

Emily looked at Devin and said, "Do you think they slept through everything last night?"

Devin shook his head yes and said, "Obviously."

They made their way into the kitchen. Emily split off to check on Garrett, and Devin grabbed a bottle of water from the cooler he had set up the day before in preparation for a power outage. Devin looked outside and already saw that Bill and Pete were sitting on a couple of pool chairs that they grabbed from Devin's staging area inside. He saw Bill get up, then popped his head in the door and said, "It's pretty nice out now. I think we are going to sit outside for a bit. Can I grab some water and maybe some juice for Pete?"

Devin looked at him in disbelief but finally said, "Sure, help yourself." Devin was going to explain that the juice in the fridge probably wasn't cold because the power had been out, but he didn't care at that point. He watched Bill grab some juice, then some water, then make his way back outside. As Bill was about to head back out, he stopped and popped his head in again and said, "By the way, what the hell happened out here?"

Devin once again looked incredulously at Bill and said, "Jack had one too many cosmoses last night."

Bill laughed and said, "Didn't we all? Fun night! Hey by the way we are going to pack up in a bit and head home." Then he went back outside to join Pete.

Devin was in shock about the horrific events of the last ten hours. His response to Bill was all he had the energy for.

What he was really thinking was that maybe Bill shouldn't have been pouring so many drinks last night. Maybe the alcohol triggered a mental illness inside Jack, and he went nuts. Maybe the possible illness lay dormant until the right combination of vodka, flirtation, and jealousy brought it to the surface. Devin was speculating, but what he witnessed and went through was not the outcome of just one too many drinks. He was certain of it.

Emily came out of the bedroom and said, "Garrett is hungry, and Dude needs to go out as well."

Devin said, "I'll take Dude out front." Devin didn't want to deal with his brother. He was angry about how everything unfolded last night, plus exhaustion was setting in and he wasn't thinking clearly. He wasn't just angry at Jack for the terror he put them through; he was angry that Bill and Pete drank too much and slept through everything. Devin needed help last night but ended up completely on his own.

Emily began fixing something for Garrett that didn't require the use of the stove or microwave. She grabbed the peanut butter and jelly and some bread and started constructing the sandwich. Devin walked Dude out the front door to begin his long, overdue pee.

Devin stood on the porch as Dude did what he had been waiting for all night in the side yard. He looked back at the door and looked closer at the gouges. It looked like a caged tiger had made them try to get out of a crate. Only the animal that made those marks was his neighbor, trying to get in. Devin looked in the bushes and saw a small plastic cover of some sort. As he inspected it further, he saw that it was an outlet cover that protected the outdoor receptacle by the porch. It was chipped and cracked and looked pretty worn. Devin recalled the various noises he heard last night and assumed Jack must have used that at one point to consistently bang on the door. He probably used that as long as he could until he found his knife that he dropped after Devin catapulted him off the porch and into the grass.
As Devin was replaying the events in his head, he looked on the street and saw the officer still sitting in his car, looking like he was filling out paperwork. He looked over at Dude, and he was still sniffing around, enjoying his freedom from

the house. When Devin looked back, he saw another patrol car pull up in front of Alan and Jack's driveway. Alan walked out of his front door immediately to greet the officer, who was now out of his car and walking around to the back door of the sedan. He opened the door and guided Jack out. He had handcuffs on, which Devin guessed was a safety precaution. Alan and the officer exchanged a few words, which was just the formality of Alan identifying Jack. The officer took a key from his belt, unlocked the handcuffs, and released Jack.

Alan and Jack made their way to their door. Devin could see how rough Jack looked. His clothes were saturated and torn. Devin could see blood stains on his shirt and arms. He wasn't sure if he cut himself with the variety of knives that now decorated the backyard or from the incessant pounding of his fist on the front door. As Jack followed Alan into the house, he stopped and looked over at Devin. The porches were close enough to one another that Devin could see his bloodshot gaze as they exchanged looks. Jack's eyes looked lifeless, almost like those of a shark. Devin immediately thought of Quint, the boat captain, from the movie 'Jaws'. He knew the lines verbatim as he ran them through his mind.

'You know the thing about a shark; he's got lifeless eyes, black eyes, like a doll's eyes. When he comes at you, he doesn't seem to be living until he bites you.'

Devin didn't show Jack any sort of emotion as he looked back. His instinct was to run over there, punch him right in the face, and watch him drop. He stopped himself, as he still saw the police officers talking in their cars. Jack turned back and walked in the door, following Alan. Devin called Dude, who had efficiently sniffed every inch of the side yard, and opened the door to go in. He looked over at Alan and Jack's house again and wondered if Jack would be capable of another episode. Was this a one-time occurrence, or could it happen again? He couldn't go down that path in his mind and quickly shook it off. He thought how strange it was that less than sixteen hours ago, they were the best neighbors they could possibly have. Now that was gone.

He knew they would be inundated with phone calls from the kids, his sisters, and the Emily family, all checking to see how they fared through the storm. As he walked in, like clockwork, Emily and Devin's phones began to ring.

CHAPTER 23

CLOSURE

Emily fielded calls from her parents and then talked to Patty. Her brother called through at one point, but it went to voicemail. She didn't want to tell the story again, so she decided to call him back later. She told Patty about what had happened, and Patty was in disbelief. Emily was just glad she wasn't here and was at least safe at college as the storm pummeled them the night before. Emily made the conscience choice not to tell her parents. Her mother was worried enough, and she didn't need to add to her stress. She would eventually tell her, but today was not the day. Emily made the call to her parents but let her father dominate the conversation as he discussed the strength of Irma, the wind speeds, and where she was currently headed.

Bill and Pete began to pack up and prepare Bella for the ride home. Devin was on the phone with Tom, explaining everything. Tom agreed with his dad that what they went through was right out of a horror movie and was in shock. Joe and Pat reacted the same way as he talked to them both on the speaker phone. Joe was over at Pats working on a project, so he was able to tell them at the same time. The consensus was complete and utter shock, but they were all glad Emily, Devin, and Garrett were okay. Emily and Devin finished the family calls and helped Bill and Pete gather their things and head out to the car. Devin was still numb and incredulous that Bill and Pete didn't really comment much when Devin told them that Jack caused the destruction outside. They seemed to be in their own world, and Devin, at that point, just wanted them gone. He needed to focus on the clean-up outside before Garrett saw anything, and he and Emily needed to rest. They walked outside to the car as Bill got Bella settled in the back seat. He turned to Devin and said, "Thanks for the hospitality, little brother." Then he gave him a hug. He turned to Emily and said, "You too, Emily," and gave her a kiss.

Pete then thanked them both and gave them hugs. Bill got behind the wheel of the car as Pete turned and insipidly said, "Good luck with your neighbor," then got in the car.

Devin looked at him and was taken aback by the flippant remark. He was too tired to react and turned to go inside with Emily. They walked into the house and gave each other a hug. Emily said, "I'm glad they are gone. I'm so tired."

Devin responded, "I totally agree on both counts. Why don't you go in with Garrett and rest with him? I'll go out and clean up the blood and grab the knives from the yard."

Devin once again couldn't believe the words that came out of his mouth. It was all so unbelievable, but it was finally over. He felt that he told Alan what he needed to say and that there was some closure as far as Jack was concerned, but it was still unsettling.

He went out back and began the clean-up while Emily went into Garrett, who was still plugging away at a video game. Devin made his way around the house and tallied all the screens that had been slashed. It was almost all of them on the bottom part of the house, except for two on the other side. He made sure he put gloves on as he scrubbed the blood-soaked windows and walls. He put all the knives in a bag and walked to the front of the house to stash them in the garage. As he walked to the front, he looked across the street and saw his neighbor, Mrs. Flemings. She was an elderly woman who loved to gossip and share stories about the neighborhood. He tried not to make eye contact with her because he was in no mood to talk. He heard her yell over, "Devin!' Devin!"

Devin couldn't avoid it any longer and responded, "Hi, Mrs. Flemings. Did you do okay with the storm?"

She quickly replied, "Yes, I think so. Just some branches down and still don't have power."

"Us too," Devin politely said, trying to end the conversation. She kept talking and said, "I saw the police there earlier. Everything ok?"

Devin knew she was fishing for gossip and answered her, "Everything is fine, Mrs. Flemings. Jack from next door had a rough night."

Devin felt a little guilty about saying something, but he didn't want her to think the police were at the house for Emily and him. Besides, he was still furious, and why should he protect Jack after what he put them through?

Mrs. Flemings said, "Wonder if he had anything to do with that?"

She pointed to her white vinyl fence. Devin saw the bloody handprints that ran down the side. He hadn't seen them earlier, when he was trying to avoid getting into a conversation with his nosey neighbor. Jack obviously made his mark as he walked through the storm on his way to the farmer's field.

"He always seemed a little off to me," Mrs. Flemings said.

She had no idea. Devin thought, then he said,
"I don't know what to tell you, Mrs. Flemings. Like I said, he had a very eventful night."

Devin hated that he was being so secretive, but he just needed this conversation to have closure. He couldn't bear living through the night again by telling the story, especially to a neighbor who would broadcast it up and down the street as soon as she could.

"Stay safe, Mrs. Flemings." Devin said, and closed the garage door.

Devin made his way into the house and saw Emily and Garrett in the kitchen. Garrett was on the couch by the window, and Emily was cleaning up a few things. Garett had his walkie-talkie by his side, and it suddenly came to life again.

"Irma central, this is Zack one," Zack said in his best authoritative tone. Garett quickly responded, "Go ahead, Zack one."

"You clear for a neighborhood inspection?" Zack asked.

Garrett looked at Emily and Devin and said, "Please? Can I go over to Zacks?"

Emily was too tired to say no and said, "Ok, but here's the deal: you should be extremely careful. There could be some branches down. You text me as soon as you get there."

Garrett jumped up as fast as he could before Emily changed her mind and raced towards the garage with his bike.

Devin looked at her and said, "He will be fine. Zack is just around the corner."

Devin knew she would worry and added the statement for extra comfort.
.
Devin and Emily stood there alone, finally. The house was quiet, and the sun was showing itself again outside. Dude was asleep on the kitchen floor, snoring away.

They both walked over to the couch and plopped down. The weight of everything they had gone through was released into the cushions of the welcome sofa. As they laid their heads back to rest, the power suddenly came back on.

All the lights that had been on last night for their little gathering were glowing again. Emily and Devin were too tired to get up and turn them off.

Devin said, "Well, that hurricane certainly rocked our world." Just then Alexa came to life and said, "*Got it. Playing Rock, You Like a Hurricane by the Scorpions*"

The speaker began to blare the 80's classic, then Emily and Devin both yelled, "Alexa, STOP."

They both laughed for a second, then closed their eyes and slept.

Bruce loved to walk on the beach with his dog, and now that he lived in Florida, it was possible every day. For the past five days, he has had to miss his routine because of Irma. His leisurely strolls along the coast and listening to podcasts were his moments of Zen each day. Today was finally the day he could get back out and pound the sand once again. Bruce had a variety of shows he would listen to and had many of them downloaded and cued in his playlist. He was also a huge environmentalist, and he would always bring a bag and some pickers with him to collect any garbage that inconsiderate tourists or lazy locals would leave behind in the sand. He knew the forecast was finally calling for sunshine that day, so he ventured out in the morning with his canine sidekick to hit

the beach. His condo building was only a block off the beach and Bruce walked over the dunes, a short walk from his apartment. He let the dog loose to go explore and play in the waves. He put his Air Pods in and cued up his next podcast, 'The Chaos Theory and Synchronicity'. He wasn't sure how he felt about the particular subject, but it was recommended by a friend and he thought he would give it a listen. He pulled out his bag to collect any debris and started his walk. Bruce could tell that the storm had stirred up a lot. The beach looked relatively quiet, and he saw only a few other people who had ventured out. Bruce began his walk and headed south along the coast. He looked down and saw a soda can and a single sock. He opened his bag, grabbed the trash with his pickers, and continued to walk. His dog was following right behind him, splashing in the waves. Bruce walked a bit further and picked up a few more unwanted items. As he stepped a few more feet, he noticed a piece of paper half buried in the sand. He reached down, pulled it out, and wiped the sand from it. It was an Eastern Caribbean dollar with a smiley face drawn on it. Bruce placed it in his pocket instead of the trash bag and continued to walk. The podcast continued to play as Bruce was only half listening to the host, who was expounding on the theories of connection, chaos theory, the butterfly effect, and synchronicity. He walked for a few more minutes when he looked down again and saw something shiny. This too was mostly buried, but Bruce used his pickers to free the item. He picked it up and noticed it was in Spanish. It was some sort of government I.D. from Guantanamo Bay. Bruce's Spanish was a little rusty, but he thought it said something about the Naval Supply Department. The picture was faded, and he could only make out the first name, Marisol. It was beat up and frayed but he placed it in the bag and moved on. Bruce continued to listen to his podcast as he watched his dog frolic in the sea and chase the seagulls that were searching for food. He walked another one hundred yards and saw another colorful piece of paper that was floating in the water. It must have just washed ashore, as it was about to be taken out to sea again. Bruce stopped it with his foot and took his pickers to grab it. He raised it up, and the card, although soggy, was still legible. He held it up, and it had a picture of a fishing boat on it. It said, Captain Barry's Fishing Charters/ Daily Excursions on board the 'Hook Em' from Key West. The phone number was faded, but Bruce could tell it was some sort of business card. He placed it in the bag and moved on. The podcast continued to play as Bruce listened to the latest segment. The host continued to talk.

"You really must wrap your head around the chaos theory. Everything is connected, and once you accept that, it becomes your reality. Chaos is the science of surprises and is unpredictable. It teaches us to expect the unexpected. It deals with things that are impossible to predict or control, like the weather, turbulence, our brain, or chaotic behavior. We could probably all figure this out if we truly understood we were connected, whether we liked it or not."

Bruce shook his head and wondered why he was listening to this. How could anyone believe in that notion, he thought? He looked up and saw that his dog was racing over to a family that was setting up their chairs and beach blankets. Bruce knew his dog could be a bit scary. He was a large German shepherd, and anyone who saw him running towards them could get the wrong idea. Bruce whistled, then yelled, "JACK! Stop!" The dog, named after Bruce's favorite actor, Jack

Nicholson, stopped in his tracks and returned to Bruce. He didn't need Jack to attack an innocent family. He decided the walk was long enough and started to head home. As he made his way back home, he saw a familiar face up ahead walking in the water. It was his neighbor, Jeffrey. As Bruce got closer to Jeffrey he said, "There he is, 'The Big Lebowski!" Bruce gave him that nickname after the character Jeffrey Lebowski from the movie. Jeffrey replied and said, "Well, hello there, shark!" That was Jeffrey's nickname for Bruce, which was also the name Steven Spielberg gave to the mechanical shark in 'Jaws'.

The two neighbors exchanged pleasantries and continued on their way. Bruce placed Jack back on the leash as he got closer to the pathway that led through the dunes back towards his condo. The podcast was just about wrapping up as the host expelled his final thoughts.

"The theory of synchronicity, developed by Swiss psychiatrist Carl Jung, suggests that meaningful coincidences are not merely random events but are instead interconnected by a deeper, meaningful relationship. According to Jung, these synchronicities reveal a connection between the inner and outer worlds, suggesting an underlying unity in the fabric of reality. The concept extends beyond the realm of cause and effect, proposing **that events** may be meaningfully related even if they lack a direct causal link. In the context of human interconnectedness, synchronicity suggests that our lives are intricately intertwined, and the events that unfold are not isolated occurrences but part of a larger, meaningful tapestry. This theory encourages a perspective that goes beyond conventional notions of cause and effect, highlighting the interconnected nature of our experiences and emphasizing *the potential for a collective, shared consciousness that binds us all together."*

Bruce chuckled again to himself, turned off the nonsense, and walked up the dune path with Jack. He came over the dunes and saw his building, The Cosmopolitan, greeting him in the distance.

EPILOGUE

Three weeks had passed, and Jack and Alan were rarely seen. Alan had texted Devin a few days after the incident to get estimates on all the damage that had been done. Devin had done his due diligence and made sure everything was taken care of and repaired. After that, there was virtually no movement at all next door. Emily came home from work one day and saw the for-sale sign on Alan and Jack's house that must have gone up while she was at work. Devin was working from home and never even saw it go up. It only took a matter of four days, and a sold sign replaced the for-sale sign. Alan and Jack must have been quietly packing inside because a week after the sale sign went up, a moving company pulled the large truck into the driveway and packed everything inside the enormous vehicle. They obviously hired a company to handle everything, and before Emily and Devin knew it, they were gone.

Emily felt a sense of sadness because they were great neighbors. Devin was still angry and hurt and still could not wrap his head around the terror that he went through, so he eventually stopped talking about it. Garett mentioned it a couple of times but eventually was distracted by so many other things that were so much more important to a ten-year-old. Devin continued to have some sleepless nights. He was trying to deal with post-traumatic stress disorder, which often triggered vivid nightmares. Some of them involved Jack actually making his way into the house. Devin would always wake up as Jack raised the knife, attempting to stab him.

Devin was still so perplexed by what triggered Jack that fateful night. He even started to listen to podcasts and read literature on the effects of hurricanes on mental health and even the chaos theory. He continued down rabbit holes until, eventually, he gave up looking for answers. All he knew was that everything changed in an instant that night, and they lost some good neighbors. They never knew where Alan and Jack moved, and frankly, Devin didn't care.

A few more weeks passed by, and the new neighbor's moving truck pulled into the driveway. Devin happened to be outside getting the mail when he saw the new neighbors approach him. They were a young couple with two little kids in tow.

Devin started the conversation. "Hi, I'm Devin. My wife is Emily, but she is at work right now. Our son Garett is at school, and our daughter is in college. We have older boys as well, but they are all on their own." Devin didn't know why he gave them the complete family history, but it was already out there.

The woman responded, "Hi, I'm Anna, and this is my husband, Beau." She pointed to the kids and said, "This is Lexi, and Troy. Devin shook Beau's hand and said, "Welcome to the neighborhood."

Beau responded, "Thanks. Hey, we are from New Mexico. We saw you guys had a busy hurricane season. Any pointers? We have never experienced one before."

Devin looked at them and said, "Just stock up, stay at home, and no cosmopolitans."

The new neighbors politely chuckled, not getting the reference, and said, "Well, let's hope we don't have to deal with any next season."

"Yeah, we can only hope," Devin said. "Well again, welcome." The new neighbors stood there awkwardly, smiling, and watched as Devin walked back into the house. As he shut the door behind him, he saw Dude sitting there waiting for him. He looked at the dog and said, "I guess someone is always watching, huh, buddy?"

Alexa then came to life and said, "Got it. Playing the 1984 hit, Somebody's Watching Me, by Rockwell."

All the speakers in the house started blaring the song. Devin went to his office, sat at his desk, and put his head down. This time, he didn't silence Alexa and let the music play.

I'm just an average man with an average life.
I work from nine to five; hey, hell, I pay the price.
All I want is to be left alone in my average home.
But why do I always feel like I'm in the Twilight Zone?
I always feel like somebody's watching me.
I always feel like somebody's watching me.
And I have no privacy.

When I come home at night, I bolt the door really tight.
People call me on the phone. I'm trying to avoid
Well, can the people really see me, or am I just paranoid?
When I'm in the shower, I'm afraid to wash my hair.
Cause when I open my eyes, I might find someone standing there.
People say I'm crazy, just a little touched.
But maybe showers remind me of "Psycho" too much.
That's why
I always feel like somebody's watching me.
I always feel like somebody's watching me.
There ain't no privacy,
It's close to midnight.
Something evil lurks in the dark.
Somebody's watching me.
Somebody's watching me.
Darkness across the land
Are the neighbors watching me?
Well, is the mailman watching me?
And I don't feel safe anymore. Oh, what a mess.
I wonder who's watching me now (who?). Is it the IRS?
I always feel like somebody's watching me.
I always feel like somebody's watching me.
You hear the door slam.
and realize there's nowhere left to run.
You feel the cold hand.
And I wonder if you'll ever see the sun.
I always feel like somebody's watching me.
I always feel like somebody's watching me.

IRMA

Hurricane Irma, a formidable Category 5 hurricane, emerged in the Atlantic on August 30, 2017, near the Cape Verde Islands. Its destructive journey began with devastating landfalls in the Caribbean, including Barbuda and St. Martin, where structures were leveled, and lives were tragically lost. Maintaining Category 5 strength for an unprecedented 37 hours, Irma then set its course towards Florida, making initial landfall in the Florida Keys on September 10, 2017, before moving up the western coast of the state. The hurricane's wrath extended to other southeastern U.S. states, causing significant damage. Though exact casualty figures varied, Irma claimed numerous lives, particularly in the Caribbean, where the storm's impact was most severe. The aftermath underscored the immense challenges of recovery and the importance of bolstering resilience in the face of increasingly powerful tropical storms.

ABOUT THE AUTHOR

With an enduring entertainment career that spans various realms and adventures, Dennis Marsico has enjoyed a continuing journey in the arts. He has performed for audiences on stage, in film, and on television. In addition to his performances, Dennis has embraced his passion for creative visions behind the scenes and now serves as a consultant for a wide array of companies, crafting, writing, and developing immersive and bespoke experiences.

Printed in the USA
CPSIA information can be obtained
at www.ICGtesting.com
CBHW081113230224
4629CB00009B/168